Understanding the
Further Education Sector

**FURTHER
EDUCATION**

You might also like the following books from Critical Publishing

A Complete Guide to the Level 4 Certificate in Education and Training
By Lynn Machin, Duncan Hindmarch, Sandra Murray and Tina Richardson
978-1-909330-89-4 September 2013

The A–Z Guide to Working in Further Education
By Jonathan Gravells and Susan Wallace
978-1-909330-85-6 September 2013

Dial M for Mentor: Critical reflections on mentoring for coaches, educators and trainers
By Jonathan Gravells and Susan Wallace
978-1-909330-00-9 In print

Most of our titles are also available in a range of electronic formats. To order please go to our Website www.criticalpublishing.com or contact our distributor, NBN International, 10 Thornbury Road, Plymouth PL6 7PP, telephone 01752 202301 or e-mail orders@nbninternational.com.

Understanding the Further Education Sector

A Critical Guide to Policies and Practices

 Susan Wallace

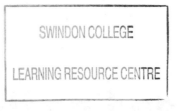
First published in 2013 by Critical Publishing Ltd

British Library Cataloguing in Publication Data

A CIP record for this book is available from the British Library

ISBN: 978-1-909330-21-4

This book is also available in the following e-book formats:

Kindle ISBN: 978-1-909330-62-7
EPUB ISBN: 978-1-909330-63-4
Adobe e-book ISBN: 978-1-909330-64-1

Cover and text design by Greensplash Limited
Project Management by Out of House Publishing
Printed and bound in Great Britain by T J International

Critical Publishing
152 Chester Road
Northwich
CW8 4AL
www.criticalpublishing.com

Contents

Meet the author

Susan Wallace

I am the Professor of Continuing Education at Nottingham Trent University, and part of my role is to support learning on the initial training courses for teachers in the Further Education sector. I taught in the sector myself for ten years, including on BTEC programmes and basic skills provision. My particular interest is in the motivation and behaviour of students in Further Education, and in mentoring and the ways in which a successful mentoring relationship can support personal and professional development. I have written a number of popular books, mainly aimed at teachers and student teachers in the sector. One aspect of this that I particularly enjoy is that it gives me opportunities to get to know lots of people, either from e-mails or in the colleges that I visit, that I wouldn't otherwise meet.

1 Introduction: the frog waiting for a kiss

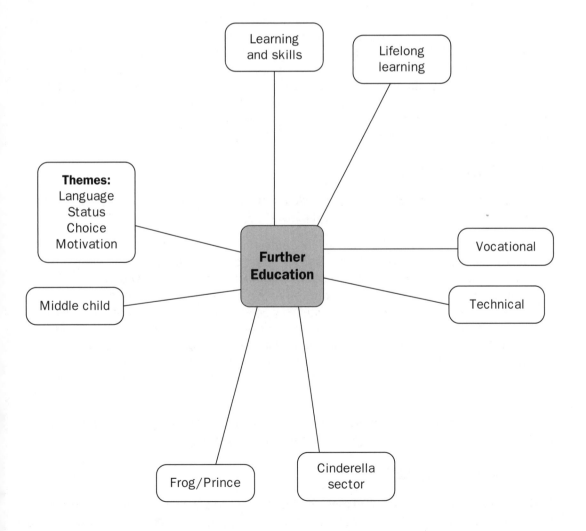

Chapter aims

This chapter is designed to help you gain an understanding of:

*   how the name of the FE sector has changed over time;

*   how the change in the sector has both reflected its role and shaped public perceptions of its purpose and status;

*   how the sector has been represented through metaphor by politicians and other policymakers and how this draws on and shapes its image in the public mind;

*   the themes and arguments covered by each chapter of the book, and how they link together.

Introduction

This chapter introduces the purpose and theme of the book, and argues that some of the over-used metaphors used to describe the sector – such as the 'Cinderella' of the education system – not only present a deficit model but also imply that there must be an easy, 'wave of the wand' way to adjust its status. If this were true, such an adjustment would surely have happened by now. The various names that have been used for the sector are also discussed here, in terms both of what these tell us about how its agreed purpose has changed over time, and how each of its aliases may have shaped public attitudes towards it, its teachers and its learners. Finally, the chapter goes on to provide a summary of those that follow, providing signposts to key themes and arguments so that the book can be navigated in a way that meets your particular needs.

Derek's farewell speech

Derek has been teaching at the same college for more than 35 years. At his retirement 'do' he makes an informal speech. Here's part of it.

> People say to me, 'How did you stick it? Being at one place all that time. Thirty-five years! What's the matter with you, Derek?' And I say to them, 'Hang on, hang on. Wait just a minute. One place? What are you talking about? Don't you believe it! I may have been here all that time, but listen: I've worked at a tech college and I've worked at a college of technology and I've worked in an FE college. And I've been a lecturer and then an assessor and then a trainer and then a teacher. And I've worked in FE and then in Vocational Education and Training; and I've worked in the Learning and Skills Sector; and I've worked in Lifelong Learning. And now I'm working in FE again. So don't tell me I've never had a change. I've had too much bloody change. I'm exhausted!'

By the time he gets to this point, everyone in his audience is laughing. They might not have put it quite like this, but they recognise exactly what he's saying.

What's in a name?

Shakespeare's Juliet argues that names don't matter. 'A rose by any other name would smell as sweet,' she says. But this chapter puts forward the opposing argument, that names *do* matter, especially in this age of advertising and spin. The way we refer to what we now call Further Education not only tells us something about the way the sector and its role is perceived, but also has the power to shape society's perception of it. Names, in other words, can both reflect *and* influence our understanding of what it is we're naming. And when it comes to names and name changes, FE has certainly had a long list for us to think about.

If we go back 50 years, we find that the institutions that offered full-time vocational courses for school leavers, and day release or evening provision for people gaining qualifications while in employment, were known as Technical Colleges. The common abbreviation for them was Techs. At the age of 15 (which was then the minimum age for leaving school) students would make their choice about whether to stay on at school to take A levels, or go to the Tech to gain the appropriate qualification for their chosen line of work. This was before the days of widespread youth unemployment, and the decision to leave school was often made because the young person wanted to begin earning a wage. From this point of view it was usually a decision based on some degree of choice, rather than a route taken through lack of other options as is frequently the case for learners entering the sector today. In Chapters 2 and 3 we'll be investigating this issue of choice – or lack of it – and the effect it may have on students' motivation and engagement with learning. But what does the name Technical College tell us about the sector? 'Technical' is a word suggestive of work that demands skills; not necessarily those of a scholarly or theoretical kind, but nevertheless important skills, involving accuracy, dexterity, expertise, ingenuity and flair. We can take 'technical', therefore, as a term that was used to differentiate this sort of education from the purely academic. The sector as a whole was known then as the Further Education sector, indicating that, for most, it followed on from school and provided learners – literally – with further education, to be distinguished from the universities and other institutions that provided degree-level higher education. The overall curriculum provided by the Tech College, however, would be described in those days as technical education.

By the late 1970s, colleges were renaming themselves, often as Colleges of Technology. Two obvious explanations for this are the shift in the economy away from heavy industry and manufacturing towards the beginnings of technological growth; and also, perhaps, the nuances of the word 'technology' itself, which suggest more of complexity, status and an eye to the future than is expressed by the merely technical. By the 1980s, however, there had been further changes of terminology; the sector was still referred to as Further Education, and the same institutions were now usually calling themselves Colleges of Further Education. This name change could be seen as quite significant. What does the transition from 'Technology' to 'Further Education' suggest about how the role of colleges at that time was developing, and what the curriculum was expected to provide? Our understanding here hinges on that word, *education*. It suggests something broader than job-specific training, a more flexible purpose than instilling technical competence or even knowledge of specialised technologies. It suggests a curriculum of equal use and value with – and offering a broad path of progression from – that of schools. Certainly FE colleges in that era were attempting to combine a vocational curriculum with elements of a *liberal* education, as we shall explore further in Chapters 2 and 5. 'Liberal' here is used in the sense of broad or general – encompassing subjects such as literature and philosophy – as opposed to purely *vocational*, which implies a narrower and functional process that focuses on developing a specific set of work-related skills. In the Further Education colleges of the 1980s, learners were still referred to as students rather than trainees; a terminology again suggesting a broader purpose than simply the acquisition of work skills. In fact the term 'trainee' came into use gradually from the 1980s onwards, first through the introduction of youth training schemes such as YTS, and later, in the 1990s, through the introduction of competence-based assessment that defined the purpose of the FE curriculum firmly as one of preparation for work and left no leeway to incorporate a broader, liberal model.

During those decades, as colleges were progressing through a series of name changes, the terminology used to describe the curriculum they offered was undergoing changes, too. In the days of the Tech College, students were said to be entering Technical Education; the word 'technical' denoting work-related skills, while 'education' indicated perhaps a continuation of the broader personal development begun in school. Over the next couple of decades it became more usual to refer to the curriculum as Vocational Education. The word 'vocational' is an interesting one – clearly work-related, but suggesting perhaps a wider range of skills now than the simply technical or manual. 'Vocation' is a word used to describe the work of priests, doctors, lawyers and teachers, for example. So, although training for these professions was clearly not being offered, the very word 'vocational' could be said to have, by association, a broader scope and suggestion of higher status work than 'technical'. In the 1980s and 1990s, with the advent of training schemes and NVQs, and the change of identity from students to trainees, the work of the sector was often referred to as Vocational Education and Training (VET). At the same time, there was always the term 'post-compulsory sector', used to indicate all post-16 provision, and also including, therefore, higher and adult education. During all subsequent upheavals, post-compulsory sector or post-compulsory education remained, and still remains, a useful synonym for FE and is usually taken to apply to that sector specifically. It seems to imply willing attendance and a route that learners follow by their own choice. However, as we shall see in Chapters 2, 3, 5 and 8, this may be a somewhat misleading impression. In 2001, the Learning and Skills Council took over the work of the Further Education Funding Council, marking another change of terminology. The FE sector was now the Learning and Skills Sector. The word 'skills', like 'technical' before it, places the emphasis firmly on meeting workforce needs.

The term Lifelong Learning Sector was introduced under the Labour governments of 1997– 2010, who set up the sector skills council, Lifelong Learning UK (LLUK) in 2005 to regulate the professional development of teachers and trainers in the sector. It's an interesting use of words, and one not confined to the UK. It reflects not only the constant need for the updating of work skills in an era of rapid technological development, but also the relative impermanence of employment in the twenty-first century, where most people can no longer expect a job for life and must expect breaks and changes in their employment, with the consequent need for upskilling or reskilling. In some European countries – Italy, for example – it is also strongly associated with adult education on a broader and more liberal model. In the UK, however, the term became closely associated with the Labour party policies; and so, with the defeat of that government in 2010, the subsequent dissolution of LLUK, and the overturning of related policies for the sector, the term 'Lifelong Learning Sector', which continues to be used elsewhere in the world, now became problematic in relation to college provision. Since then the term 'Further Education' has crept back into use. Of course, we could say it never really went away. It always remained the term most people used when talking about colleges. Whatever the colleges or the sector were calling themselves at the time, FE college was a name that seemed to stick.

Does all this matter? Well, yes, it really does. The language we use, or are encouraged to use, as well as shaping how we see things, can also reveal a lot about our shared values and attitudes. For example, think about the word 'master'. What do you associate with this? Mastery, perhaps; or leadership. Now consider the word 'mistress'. All we have done is to change the gender; but notice the difference in values and attitudes associated with it. You can see the same thing with the words 'bachelor' with its positive connotations of freedom and fun, and 'spinster'. They are both words to describe unmarried people, but they are value-laden in very different ways. When the Conservative party came to power in 2010 they created a Ministry of FE, Skills and Lifelong Learning. It's a lovely example of hedging the bets. 'Skills' satisfies some because it signals that it's about preparation for work; 'FE' satisfies those who believe it should not be simply instrumental, not only about preparation for work; and 'Lifelong Learning' appears to preserve – for the time being – the status quo. This matter of language can be unintentionally comical, too. John Hayes, who headed that ministry, delivered an early speech to representatives of colleges in which he deployed the words 'learning', 'education' and 'training' interchangeably when speaking about the FE curriculum. This choice of vocabulary was meant, perhaps to signal his support for the principle of parity between vocational and academic routes, that both were equally to do with learning and education, even if FE focuses most on training. However, he reportedly went on to say: 'I've done some bricklaying today. I want to live the job.'

Critical Thinking Activity 1

» *At the beginning of this chapter we heard from an FE teacher, Derek, looking back on the changes he's seen during his career. Think about how you could find out how the name and mission of your own college has changed over the past few decades, and how those changes have affected the working lives of its teachers.*

» *Now consider the following pairs of words and identify the difference in terms of the ideas and status associated with each.*

a) *student – trainee*

b) *lecturer – trainer*

c) *examination – test*

d) *teach – deliver*

» *What conclusions would you draw from this about the vocabulary of education and training?*

The fairy tale sector

One of the most famous descriptions of the FE sector is the one given in a speech by Kenneth Baker in 1989 when he referred to it as the 'Cinderella' sector. What he may have meant by this is that the sector had been, up until that time, neglected in favour of its two sisters, compulsory schooling and higher education; but that it was, potentially, the most promising of the three and would soon come into its own. All it needed was a fairy godmother to give it the wherewithal – in this case, presumably, adequate funding – and tell it, 'You *shall* go to the ball!' So, was Kenneth Baker describing himself as a fairy godmother? It seems unlikely. And, in any case, FE didn't appear any the better off at the end of Baker's stint as

Education Secretary than it had at the beginning. And was it really likely that he was claiming FE's status, given half the chance, could outshine schools and universities? That seems a bit unlikely, too. But when you use a metaphor, like this one about Cinderella, you must expect people to unpack it. A metaphor is a figure of speech where a resemblance between two things is implied by using one to stand for the other. 'He's a pig' is a good example. It's saying 'he' looks or behaves (or smells or eats) like a pig. But it's not to be taken literally. He's not *actually* a pig (unless you're pointing to a pig when you say it, obviously). So when Baker calls FE the Cinderella of the education sector, we are justified in exploring just what the resemblance is that he's drawing our attention to. Cinderella does all the mucky work, gets her hands dirty, while her sisters swan about. She has the lowest status in the household; her poverty is obvious from her outward appearance – no finery for her. And it's all very unfair. Is *this* what he means? We'll never know for sure. But it went down well at the time. The FE sector took it to indicate that it had gained some recognition at last and that good times were on their way. But such things are never achieved by the wave of a wand; and in some ways we could see Baker's use of the Cinderella metaphor as typical of politicians' rhetoric. It was astute in that it won approval, but profoundly misleading in suggesting that there was any magical quick fix that would in a flash raise the status of the FE sector and give it parity of esteem with universities.

In 2005 we were offered a different metaphor. Foster, in his report, *Realising the Potential: A Review of the Future Role of Further Education Colleges* (2005) described FE as the 'middle child' of the education system, occupying its position between schools (younger) and higher education (older). He seems to have been drawing here on the idea that the middle child of a family is often overlooked or neglected – a theory that has entered the popular imagination and seems most often subscribed to these days by middle siblings looking for a bit of sympathy over their third pint. Foster's middle child has obvious elements in common with Baker's Cinderella. Both draw on the idea of neglect and of a hopeless rivalry with others who should be viewed as equals but are in practice – and quite unfairly – both better loved and more valued. Under careful scrutiny, each of these metaphors looks very much like just another deficit model of FE, but disguised as something else – a show of concern, perhaps; or an expression of solidarity. In Chapter 4 we'll be exploring further how the language of metaphor has been used to shape and reflect our perceptions of FE; and how it sometimes gives us clues to the real attitudes behind the rhetoric of policy documents and public statements. Meanwhile, if we have to think of FE in terms of fairy tales, I'd rather present it as the frog in *The Princess and the Frog*, a useful creature who rescues the princess's ball from a well and in return asks only to be fed from her plate and to share her pillow and be shown that he is loved. Of course, when this happens he turns into a handsome prince. Just so, FE is only waiting to be cared for, given equal rights and treated with respect before it will be transformed before our very eyes into a sector of high status and well-deserved reputation. In other words, it's a frog just waiting to be kissed. The only difficulty is that its current image may exclude it from the very embrace – in terms of policy reform – necessary to transform it.

Critical Thinking Activity 2

FE has also been referred to as 'the sector of the second chance'.

» *What do you understand this to mean?*

»   *In your view, how accurate is this as an image of FE?*

»   *What positive aspects or functions of the sector does it convey?*

»   *Could this phrase also have negative associations, and if so, what might they be?*

Finding your way around this book

You will find that the way FE provision has evolved over the decades, and the role of language and metaphor in shaping and reflecting its purpose and status are two of the recurring themes in this book. Chapter 2 explores the sector's ancestry from the nineteenth century onwards, showing how and why we have arrived at the sort of college and curriculum we have today. It looks particularly at the question of FE's status in relation to school or to higher education, and explains where some of the ideas about its value and purpose have come from. Chapter 3 takes a close look at how the vocational qualification structure has developed and – importantly – how it has shaped, and continues to shape, the role and identity of teachers in the FE sector. It explores the arguments about parity between vocational and general or 'academic' qualifications, and presents the debates around sector specific qualifications for teachers. In Chapter 4 we pick up the topic of language again and analyse some of the discourses about FE that can be found in policy documents such as government White Papers on education and training. Here we find metaphors being used that sometimes seem to contradict the surface rhetoric.

Chapter 5 turns to the world of fiction and takes a look at how FE is portrayed in novels and on television, and what that tells us about how the sector is perceived in the popular imagination. It looks particularly at the question of status, not just in relation to the sector as a whole but also to its learners and its teachers. Then, in Chapter 6, we take a look at what life in an FE college looks like from the perspective of the newcomer, by seeing what trainee teachers find most striking or memorable about their first few weeks of teaching experience. We see how situations can be interpreted and misinterpreted; and how reflection on what is observed can be used to develop future practice. Following this, in Chapter 7, we pull some of our themes together and look at the arguments for and against broadening the vocational curriculum by introducing elements of a more general education. We explore the various attempts to do this in the past, and look at the outcomes; and we consider the implications of a progressively narrowing curriculum. Chapter 8 draws together the elements of another major theme, which is about the motivation, engagement and behaviour of young FE learners. We look at the main issues that arise for teachers, and the strategies teachers use to address them. We also consider the extent to which the motivation of learners is within the teacher's power to influence, and how far it might be considered an institutional or sector-wide issue. In Chapter 9 we hear from learners themselves; from leaders and managers; and from teachers, some with many years of experience of teaching in the sector. We see what they have to say on the subjects that form the themes of this book: the role and status of FE; the language we use about it; the nature of its curriculum; and the sense of identity of its teachers and learners. Chapter 10, the final chapter, summarises the themes and arguments and looks at how they can be incorporated into essays, assignments and projects in order to provide context and demonstrate understanding. It then looks at possible ways forward, both at a practical level for individual teachers and managers, and also at a policy level for the sector as a whole. In other words, it offers some answers to the question: how do we make sure the frog gets a kiss?

Chapter reflections

We have explored here:

» The way that our choice of words and how we name the sector and its colleges both reflect society's attitude towards them, and influence society's understanding of them.

» How the terminology used to describe the sector and its colleges has changed over time, and the implications of these changes.

» How the best known metaphors for FE – the 'Cinderella sector' and the 'middle child' – fail to imply any realistic way to improve the sector's status.

» The suggestion that the fairy tale of the frog prince is a more apposite metaphor, presenting FE as a sector whose traditional image may deter the kiss – in terms of policy reform – needed to transform it.

» How the themes and arguments of the book can be followed through the succeeding chapters.

Taking it further

If you'd like to read more about how words can both form and reflect society's values and attitudes, you may enjoy the following, from which the examples of master/mistress and bachelor/spinster were taken. This is quite an old book, but a classic of its kind. Spender is writing specifically about sexism and language; but her argument is relevant to any consideration of how expressions of status and value are implicit in the vocabulary we use.

Spender, D. (1980) *Manmade Language*. London: Routledge and Kegan Paul.

References

Foster, A. (2005) *Realising the Potential: A Review of the Future Role of Further Education Colleges*. Annesley: DfES.

2 Parity or prejudice? The origins and purpose of FE

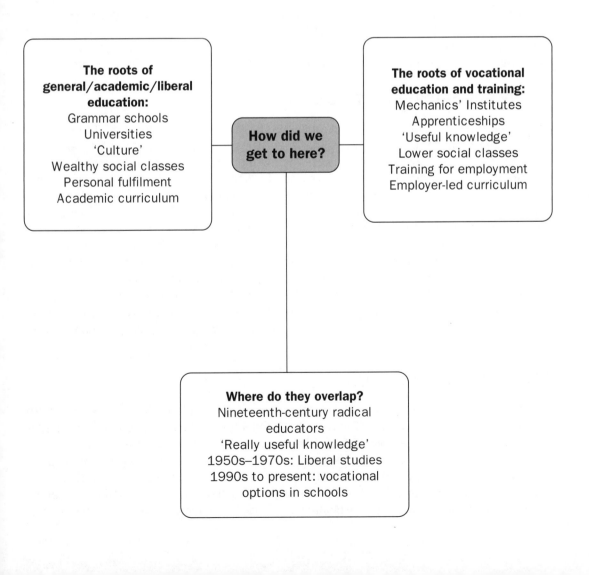

The roots of general/academic/liberal education:
Grammar schools
Universities
'Culture'
Wealthy social classes
Personal fulfilment
Academic curriculum

How did we get to here?

The roots of vocational education and training:
Mechanics' Institutes
Apprenticeships
'Useful knowledge'
Lower social classes
Training for employment
Employer-led curriculum

Where do they overlap?
Nineteenth-century radical educators
'Really useful knowledge'
1950s–1970s: Liberal studies
1990s to present: vocational options in schools

Chapter aims

This chapter is designed to help you gain an understanding of:

• the origins of the Further Education sector;

• the factors that have shaped its role and status up to the present day;

• how assumptions about the purpose of Further Education have changed over time.

Introduction

Exploring the origins of our present-day Further Education sector is rather like researching a family tree. In this chapter we're going to look at the sector's ancestry, from its origins in the nineteenth century to its current role and function, and see how successive policies and beliefs about society, education and the economy have shaped it into what we know today. As well as the idea of the family tree, it will be useful to keep in mind two other images while reading this chapter. One is a game board, which we might call, perhaps, What's Your Future? or The Education and Training Game. The other is the idea of a time-traveller, tracking the aims and status of vocational education and training across the centuries. With these pictures in mind we're going to discuss the sometimes surprising assumptions that have routinely been made about the educational and training needs of the sector's learners.

The Mechanics' Institutes

So let's start by going back to a direct ancestor of today's Further Education (FE) Colleges: the Mechanics' Institutes. These were set up in the second quarter of the nineteenth century and were initially seen as a means of meeting the aspirations of the working classes to education and self-improvement. Workers who had been forced to earn a wage since childhood and who had little or no formal schooling were able to attend their local institute in the evenings at the end of their long working day in order to learn and to 'improve' themselves. These Mechanics' Institutes, however, also served the purposes of employers who, in the rapidly expanding industrial economy of the nineteenth century, needed a workforce sufficiently skilled to work the machines and keep the ledgers. This employment-driven aspect of the curriculum was referred to as 'useful knowledge', and was promoted by a body called the Society for the Diffusion of Useful Knowledge (SDUK). The suspicion that the institutes, rather than promoting social mobility and educational opportunity, were in fact a means of creating a skilled but docile workforce fuelled the growth of a movement known as the Radical Educators.

The Radical Educators

The Radical Educators feared that the education being offered to workers was simply a process of indoctrination that, far from promoting intellectual inquiry, was actually designed to stifle it so as to discourage workers from questioning their own lack of power and status and their meagre wage. Another problem with the concept of 'useful knowledge' or education as preparation for work was that it was easily open to abuse and exploitation by unscrupulous individuals and institutions. Charles Dickens, who was a great enthusiast for the Mechanics' Institutes, savagely lampoons this exploitative attitude to vocational training with his account of Mr Squeers' approach to teaching in the novel *Nicholas Nickleby*. Headmaster Squeers asks a boy, 'What is a horse?' When the boy answers that it is a beast (in other words, an animal), Squeers announces that the boy now has sufficient knowledge and sends him to put it to practical use by grooming Squeers' horse. This portrayal of oppression and exploitation masquerading as education illustrates vividly for us the criticisms levelled at the proponents of 'useful knowledge' or vocational education in the first half of the nineteenth century.

'Useful knowledge'

In challenging the concept of useful knowledge the Radical Educators instigated a wider debate about the purposes of education and about what it means to be educated. The key question they raised about the idea of useful knowledge was: 'useful for whom?' The answer, they argued, was almost certainly not the working man or woman, but those employers who needed a trained workforce to operate the machines that were creating wealth for their owners. The Radical Educators ridiculed the SDUK and the whole idea of 'provided education'; that is, education set up by employers or the state, which comes with its own hidden agenda of social control. And they offered instead a curriculum that they described pointedly as 'really useful knowledge'. This addressed three main areas of learning: political knowledge aimed at bringing about social change; social science informed by secularism, feminism and social co-operation; and an examination of the questions of poverty and exploitation. It is easy to understand how these ideas were seen at the time as radical and even dangerous. And we can see, too, that this sort of curriculum – one that challenges and asks questions about society and the individual's place in it – is quite different from a curriculum designed to equip the learner with the skills necessary to make him or her a useful component of the workforce. In this conflict of ideas between the proponents of 'useful knowledge' and the Radical Educators with their 'really useful knowledge' we can see the origins of that distinction that has been the subject of so much debate in the Further Education sector: the dividing line between training and education; or the difference between a vocational and a general (sometimes called 'academic') education.

Education? What did they mean?

To understand the implications of this conflict fully, we need to go back a little and look at what was commonly understood by the term 'education' in the early to mid-nineteenth century. What we find is something very different – and much narrower – than our present-day understanding. A formal education was largely restricted to the moneyed classes and usually meant a knowledge of the classics, including the grammar and literature of Latin and ancient Greek. It was also to a very great extent gender-specific, its purpose being to produce gentlemen of culture. Women of the same class (who would certainly insist on being called 'ladies') were usually expected to acquire skills more appropriate to their decorative status, such as embroidery, sketching or playing the piano. Of course, it was recognised that a wider understanding of more practical matters, such as science and mechanics, was necessary to meet the needs of the rapidly expanding mechanisation on which the country's progress depended; but this was not considered an area of knowledge necessary for gentlemen. To acquire such knowledge would imply the need to work for a living and to work for a living was inconsistent with a gentleman's status. It was more fitting that such subjects, which fell outside the definition of 'culture', should be left to the skilled working class or artisans – the 'mechanics' of the Mechanics' Institutes – leaving gentlemen to maintain a dignified distance from such 'useful knowledge' that related to the world of work, industry and labour. And so, as a result, we again see two different purposes of education being identified, with the division here falling directly along the lines of social class.

Education versus working for a living

This distinction between a cultured education on the one hand and learning that is useful for the world of work on the other is particularly clear in some of the government-commissioned reports of the time, especially that of the Clarendon Commission of 1864 and the Taunton Commission of 1868. The report of the Clarendon Commission described the exclusion of science from the curriculum of major public schools as *a great practical evil*, but then went on to say that the role these schools played in maintaining classical Greek and Latin as the mainstay of an English education *far outweighs the error of having clung to these studies too exclusively*. In other words, science should be recognised as an important subject for study, but its absence from the curriculum could be forgiven as long as Greek and Latin were given due emphasis. What this meant in practical terms was that the major public schools were able to continue with their curriculum of the classics to the exclusion of science or any other subject that could be remotely connected to the world of work; and the minor public schools, eager to emulate them, did the same.

In the report of the Taunton Commission that followed four years later we see a clear hierarchical ranking of educational needs according to social class. There are, the report claims, three grades of parents. The first are those who want their children to continue in school up to and beyond the age of 18, and who want to keep Latin and Greek as the mainstay of an English education. These parents:

> have nothing to look to but education to keep their sons on a high social scale. And they would not wish to have what might be more readily converted into money if in any degree it tends to let their children sink in the social scale.
> (Report of the Taunton Commission, quoted in Maclure, 1986, p 93)

Critical Thinking Activity 1

» What do you think the report means by *what might be more readily converted into money? What is the report saying here? How does this argument fit into what we have learned so far about education, social class and the origins of the Further Education sector?*

Education, work and social class

The Taunton Report was expressing the view, widely held at the time, that an education that was designed to equip the learner to earn a living was inappropriate for the offspring of the higher social classes; and that to provide them with an education that could be described as 'useful' in this respect would be to lower their social standing. For those at the top of the social order, as we've seen, education was not about work but about acquiring culture. Further down the social scale, parents described by the report as 'second grade' would want their children to be educated to about the age of 16 and to gain a grounding in Latin, but also to acquire a knowledge of practical subjects useful for the world of business. Even this, however, would include very little that we today would call 'vocational'. The subjects they would study would be English, mathematics, natural science and perhaps a foreign language. Lower still on the social scale were the 'third grade' parents. They would probably, according to the report, keep their children in education to the age of 14, an education that would not involve the study of classics but only reading, writing and arithmetic – key skills for employment in those days as they are today. And beneath these three grades would of course be the majority – the children of the poor and the underclass who would still be unlikely to receive much formal education, if any at all.

What the Taunton Report of 1868 shows us very clearly is how closely educational provision 150 years ago was linked in the national perception to notions about social class; and how curriculum subjects acquired status the further removed they were from the world of work. At the same time it shows us how prestige was attached to a lengthy education in school, and how conclusions about social status might be drawn from the age at which an individual finished their school education.

Critical Thinking Activity 2

» *Think about the Further Education sector today. How does the status of its learners and its qualifications compare to that of a local sixth form or, in the case of its degree level work, to a local university? Can you identify any similarities between the ideas and assumptions expressed in the Taunton Report 150 years ago and attitudes towards vocational qualifications today? Can you think of at least three ways in which attitudes and assumptions about vocational education and general education are different today to those of the mid-nineteenth century?*

What today's sector has inherited

So far, in researching the family tree of FE, we have discovered the history of two significant ideas that continue even now to influence attitudes towards the sector. Both are bound up in beliefs about status and class.

- First there is the notion that education or training that is aimed directly at preparation for work is somehow less prestigious than a general or academic education; so that acquiring skills in plumbing and acquiring skills in Latin each carries with it vestiges of ideas about status, worth and class. The fact that to most of us a knowledge of plumbing is probably the more useful of the two does not automatically challenge people's preconceptions about its relative status. In fact, as we have seen, historically it was that very usefulness that devalued it.

- Second there is the notion that a lengthy general education is synonymous with high social class. We think of those 'first class' parents, so called by the Taunton Report, who kept their sons in school beyond the age of 18; and then we think of today's equivalent who would be parents of teenagers who stay on in the sixth form, taking A levels with a view to going on to university. When it comes to a question of whether a young person stays on in the sixth form or leaves school at 16 and goes to college, it seems that judgements about value and status are still, even today, attached to this decision.

Leaving school at the first opportunity and choosing to train directly for work is the route taken by many learners we encounter in the sector and particularly those in FE colleges. But, as we've seen, this combination carries with it generally unexamined notions from the nineteenth century about worth and social standing. While this certainly provides us with an explanation for the so-called 'Cinderella' status of the sector, perhaps more importantly it provides us with a challenge too, and encourages us to think about what we can do to bring about a change in perceptions and values.

Critical Thinking Activity 3

In the previous paragraph you'll have noticed again the reference to Further Education as the Cinderella sector. As we saw in Chapter 1, this was a phrase used by Kenneth Baker in his role as Secretary of State for Education in 1989, and it was one that stuck. More recently the sector was described in the Foster Report (2005) as the middle child *of the education system. Take some time to reflect on the implications of these metaphors. Consider particularly:*

» *how each of them relates to what we have learnt so far in this chapter about the sector's origins and status;*

» *what each of these metaphors implies about the future and future status of the sector;*

» *how the language we choose to use, and the language we hear, about the Further Education sector both forms and reflects our ideas about its role and its value;*

» *who or what, by implication, might be the ugly sisters or the oldest and youngest children? How well do these Cinderella and middle child metaphors really work when we begin to unpack them?*

» *what alternative metaphors could be used to describe FE? (Mine, you'll remember, was the frog waiting to be kissed. How well does this work, do you think?)*

Apprenticeships

The next branch of the family tree we're going to look at is even older and goes a long way back to a model of learning that survived for many centuries and was widely respected. In medieval times skilled craftsmen such as silversmiths, stonemasons, blacksmiths and potters passed on their skills and knowledge by taking on apprentices who served seven years learning the craft from their master until they could be considered independent skilled craftsmen in their own right. Families paid a fee for their sons to become 'qualified' in this way, and an agreement would be drawn up between the apprentice (or his family) and the master. Few people at this social level would be able to read, so the agreement would often be torn in half, the apprentice retaining one half and the master the other. The legal proof of their agreement could be ascertained by seeing that the two halves fitted and matched. It was a contract in which the master undertook to teach and the apprentice committed himself to learn.

In this traditional apprenticeship model we can see a forerunner of concepts and practices that are familiar today, such as work-based learning, individualised learning, work experience, mentoring and one-to-one tutorials. It was a model that survived well into the second half of the twentieth century; and it would be natural to assume that today's apprenticeships are a direct descendant of this centuries-old approach to training. This, however, is not the case. In the 1980s there was a break in the line of descent and the apprenticeships we have today – although they've been given the old family name – have a different origin altogether, as we shall see in the final section of this chapter.

Equality of opportunity? The Butler Act

If we imagine our time-traveller now, moving towards us out of the nineteenth century and into the twentieth, we see them passing through important landmark dates in the history of educational provision, marked by the passing of successive Education Acts:

* 1870: school boards are created to fund schooling for children of the poor.

* 1880: compulsory schooling is introduced for all children up to the age of ten.

* 1918: compulsory schooling age is raised to 14.

Nevertheless, inequalities of educational opportunity continued, and towards the end of the Second World War an attempt was made to address these. It took the shape of the 1944 Education Act, often referred to as the Butler Act after R.A. Butler (1902–1982), who was President of the Board of Education at the time – we'd call him Minister for Education today – and who was credited with devising the reforms contained in the act. These included establishing the three phases of education: primary, secondary and Further Education; the raising of the school leaving age to 15; and the introduction of the 11-plus exam taken by all children in their final year of primary education. Based on their performance in this test, children were selected to go on to one of three types of secondary schooling – grammar, modern or technical schools – according to what were judged to be their abilities, needs and aptitudes. Grammar schools provided for those children who performed best in the 11-plus examination. The curriculum of the grammar schools included – as we might guess from our knowledge of their nineteenth-century counterparts – Latin and sometimes ancient Greek, modern foreign languages, literature, science and the whole range of subjects that we still associate with an academic curriculum. It provided for learners up to the age of 18. The curriculum of the technical schools placed a broad emphasis on technical or science-based subjects; and the modern schools – or secondary moderns as they came to be called – offered practical subjects such as woodwork or sewing, alongside the required subjects of reading, writing and arithmetic. Schooling for these pupils ended at the age of 15.

The philosophy behind this tri-partite (three part) system was that it was possible to identify at the age of 11 a person's aptitudes, skills and level of intelligence, and therefore to provide them with an education best suited to their needs. In the wording of this 1944 act we encounter a phrase that has become familiar to those of us who are involved with the Further Education sector: *parity of esteem*. It was claimed that the three types of schooling would be of equal status and that the education each provided would be valued equally by society as a whole. Alas, this was not the case. Before very long it became the norm to speak about the 11-plus in terms of 'passing' it or 'failing' it. Pass it, and you gained access to a grammar school education with all the advantages this implied, including the possibility of progressing to university. Fail it (that is, fail to get a grammar school place), and a whole range of possibilities became closed to you in terms of higher education and employment. The problem was that although it did open up the possibility of social mobility and a university education for some high achieving children from working-class backgrounds, the tri-partite or 11-plus system was still based on ideas about work, class and culture that are not so far removed from those we saw in the previous century.

Critical Thinking Activity 4

» *Thinking back over what you've read in this chapter so far, what parallels can you see between the education and training provision described in the Taunton Report of 1868 and the provision laid out in the Butler Act of 1944? Are there any ideas or assumptions that are common to both?*

» *One concept that clearly informs them both is the principle of selection. Take some time to reflect on your own views about selection. Is it necessary? Is it desirable? What purpose does it serve? At what stage or stages in the education and training system should it occur, if at all? Is the age of 11 too young? Why or why not, and what might be a better age? Thinking back over your own time in education, as a learner and as a teacher, have you yourself experienced, observed or implemented selection? How has this informed your views?*

A century later...

Let's move down the family tree now to 1968, 100 years after the Taunton Report, and see which traits of the sector's nineteenth-century ancestors were carried forward into relatively modern times. By this point, Further Education and vocational training provision in Britain had become an integral part of the education system. Much of the provision was delivered through 'technical colleges' under the aegis of the local education authorities, which also ran the schools, so that each area's local education provision from five to 18-plus was strategically managed, funded, advised and inspected. This meant that, instead of competition between local schools and colleges and between one local college and another, there could be collective collaboration and strategically planned and funded provision. Where one college might offer courses in construction, for example, but have no engineering provision, another could be well-resourced for engineering but offer no provision in construction. In this way, local areas provided the learner with a wide choice of provision shared across a number of institutions. The local education authorities were also responsible for the polytechnics, institutions of higher education that offered degree level courses in vocational subjects. University places in those days were limited, and entrance to them was almost exclusively via high grade A levels. The polytechnics, therefore, provided an alternative progression route to higher education that was also accessible to those students from the technical colleges who had the appropriate qualifications. What we see here, then, 100 years after the Taunton Report, is a model that reflects a far greater degree of social mobility. There is compulsory education for all up the age of 15 (it wasn't raised to 16 until 1973), with the option – for those who don't choose to stay on at school – to progress to a free, structured and publicly funded provision of vocational education and training up to degree level. And one important factor we must bear in mind about vocational training at this time is that there was no shortage of jobs. School leavers at 16 years old could be reasonably confident of finding a job. And if it was in a vocational area that required specific skills, it was quite usual for the employer to pay for a course at the local technical college and release the employee one day a week or more, with pay, to attend. This arrangement was known as 'day release'.

Nevertheless, there is still plenty that a time-traveller from the nineteenth century would recognise. Apprenticeships are still around in 1968, and still operating on a time-served basis; although the apprentice's contract is likely to be with a firm rather than with an individual master craftsman, and he or she (but still mainly he), too, will probably be attending the technical college one day a week to learn the theory that underpins the practicality of the craft or trade. An alternative option for workers to gain or improve their qualifications was attendance after work at evening classes. College attendance for employees was generally seen by employers as an investment that would help provide them with skilled and well-qualified workers who would be an asset to their business. What they were learning was 'useful knowledge'.

We can also hear a distant echo of the Mechanics' Institutes in the term 'technical college'. The word 'institute' was still around too. It was not uncommon for vocational and adult evening classes and their venue at the technical college to be referred to still as an 'evening institute'. And also, interestingly, the debate about the purpose and nature of education and training was still evident within the curriculum of technical colleges themselves – a curriculum that in many instances had developed to combine work-related skills and knowledge with elements of a cultural or liberal education. It's important to understand that 'liberal' in this context doesn't relate in any way to party politics. It is a word used to describe an education that aims to equip the learner with an understanding of their own culture and an ability to appreciate and enjoy literature, art, architecture, history and similar areas of knowledge considered to be enriching and life-enhancing. A liberal education is a broad education, the sort of education we saw those 'first class' gentlemen receiving a century before. It is not instrumental in the sense in that it will not train you directly in specific vocational skills; the vocational curriculum will do that. But it might well provide you with what we would call today 'transferable skills': the ability to distinguish fact from opinion, a higher level of literacy, an enjoyment of learning and a wider horizon for your career ambitions. This curriculum enrichment was provided in the form of liberal studies, which formed an hour or two of the weekly timetable for most vocational students, both day release and full-time.

Our time-traveller from the 1860s would probably recognise these two curriculum elements as a combination of ideas from both sides of the debate about what constitutes useful knowledge: knowledge and skills that fitted the learner for work and met the needs of employers; and a wider, more general range of knowledge and skills that encouraged an informed engagement with society and culture and learning. In the 1960s the liberal studies part of the curriculum took various forms but often included discussion of modern fiction, television or advertising; an understanding of how forces such as the police or fire services operated; consumers' rights; employment law; and so on.

So, over the century, there had been great changes, although some elements of vocational education and training remained recognisable. But what about those two nineteenth-century ideas that we identified in the first section of this chapter: the belief that education or training that is aimed directly at preparation for work is somehow less prestigious than a general or academic education; and the idea that a lengthy general education is an indication of higher social class? Well, sadly, a century later these notions were still around and still informing perceptions about vocational education and the technical colleges that provided it. Prestige was still attached to a lengthy schooling. Students who stayed on at school to study A levels with a view to qualifying for university were widely regarded as more 'successful' or 'brighter' than those who left at 16 and trained for work. There were far fewer universities in those days, and so competition for places was high; perhaps only one in 30 young people could expect to succeed. University was the target destination in an intensely selective education system, and statistics from that time show that social class was a significant predictor of children's success, with those from middle-class homes being more likely to remain in school beyond the age of 16 and to gain a place at university than their working-class contemporaries. Or, to put this another way, students from working-class homes were more likely to leave school at 16 and attend technical colleges than students from a middle-class background. This had the effect of positioning colleges and their vocational training provision firmly in a class context. Further Education was often referred to (and sometimes still is) as the sector of the second chance – the sector that provides learning opportunities for those who didn't succeed in school the first time around. In a system where 'success' was measured in O levels (the forerunners of GCSEs), A levels and university degrees, this attitude was perhaps inevitable.

Playing the game

Let's leave family trees and time-travellers for a moment and imagine the education and training situation up to this point as a big board game along the lines of Monopoly or Game of Life. Let's call it The Education and Status Game. What would it look like? Well, in the earliest version of the game – say 1868 – very few people would even have been allowed to play. Those who were would begin by picking a card that allocated them their role. According to whether they drew the first class, second class, third class or apprentice card they would have a fixed route around the board. The routes would all diverge from the first throw of the dice and would lead to different destinations. Nothing the players did would change their route once their role card was drawn. And only the route taken by the player with the 'first class' card would lead to the winning post, every time. It wouldn't be a very interesting game because it would always be obvious from the beginning who would win.

The game would become a little more interesting after 1944. For one thing, education up to the age of 15 was compulsory by then and so everyone could play. To begin with, players would all shake dice to race with one another along the same track on the board. But about halfway around the board the track would fork into three possible routes. Players would be required to stop and draw an '11-plus card' that would direct them which fork to take. Comparatively few cards would be printed with 'pass and go to grammar school'. But the grammar school route would be the only one that led directly to the winning post. The other two routes may have got you there in the end, but only long after the lucky winner has been declared.

The analogy of the game board is a useful one because it allows us to take a step back and look at the situation analytically. We see, for example, the principle of selection playing a very important role; and also the way in which life choices become narrowed or predetermined at an early age. We see, too, how the 'academic' route leads to the winning post every time as long as a sixth form education at school remains the goal.

Critical Thinking Activity 5

» *We still hear GCE A levels referred to by politicians and others as the 'gold standard'. Can you think of other ways in which the Education and Status Game of today resembles the 1968 version? In what ways has it changed, do you think? How would the board look today? Take some time to think about this before going on to read the next section.*

1986–1992: All change!

Major changes to the vocational curriculum took place in the 1980s. A government White Paper called *A New Training Initiative* appeared in 1981 setting out three main proposals. One argued for a one-year work-related training scheme for all 16-year-old school leavers. This was eventually to lead to the creation of the Youth Training Scheme (YTS). Another proposal was for the setting up of training courses for unemployed adults, designed to equip them with the skills that employers were looking for. Up to this point, most people in vocational education were either already employed or were undertaking recognised qualifications with a realistic hope, if they worked hard and passed their exams, of gaining employment in their chosen vocational area. The creation of the training schemes instigated an era of what has been called *training without jobs* (Finn, 1987). The question for teachers was now to become: how do we motivate learners who have no promise of that reward even if they work hard on this scheme and demonstrate punctuality and good behaviour? How do we answer their question, 'What's the point?' if there are no jobs for them at the end of the scheme? The declared purpose of the training schemes was to equip people with the skills that employers wanted. They are therefore based on a deficit model of the learner. In other words they imply that the reason learners are unemployed is because they lack – are deficient in – the sort of skills that employers are looking for. For many critics of the schemes this was seen as a way of drawing attention away from the wider economic and political causes of rising unemployment.

The third proposal was to replace the traditional time-serving apprenticeship with competence-based qualifications. And for other vocational qualifications, too, the emphasis was no longer to be on time served – that is, attendance on a course for a year or two years culminating in an end exam – but on an assessment of competence. Put simply: if you could do it, no matter when you could do it, you got the qualification. This policy proposal led to the introduction, in 1986, of the National Vocational Qualification Framework into which all existing vocational qualifications offered by a range of awarding bodies including City and Guilds, BTEC and the Royal Society of Arts were expected to fit. In order to have their qualifications endorsed by the National Council for Vocational Qualifications (NCVQ) and become accepted NVQs within the national framework, awarding bodies were required to adapt and present their specifications for approval in a competence-based format.

Critical Thinking Activity 6

Let's stop there for a moment and consider the implications of all this for the sector. If apprenticeships were to be discontinued and if trainees did not have to attend courses but only had to be tested for competence, what did this mean for the role of the teacher? Would teaching give way to assessment as the main activity of the sector's staff? Would colleges themselves become more like MOT centres, with people passing through to be assessed for their level of competence and awarded a certificate if they passed? Both of these were real fears expressed at the time. Of course, in most cases the teacher's work and the functioning of the college did not undergo quite so radical a transformation. But nevertheless the introduction of competence-based qualifications did bring about changes in the way teachers in the sector saw their role, and in the way their role was perceived by others. One interesting example is that up to this point it had been usual to refer to them as 'lecturers' – perhaps because their students were young adults rather than of school age. The title drew attention to what they had in common with their counterparts in universities. But the idea of lecturing is not really compatible with a competence-based assessment role and, over time, we've seen the terms teacher, tutor or trainer become more commonly used.

» *With this in mind, what other implications arising from the introduction of NVQs can you identify in relation to the role and status of the sector?*

» *What happens to the notion of liberal education in a competence-based system?*

» *Now consider the introduction of training schemes for school leavers and for adults. What impact do you think this may have had on the role of the teacher and of the college as a whole?*

You may be wondering how, if apprenticeships were discontinued in the 1980s, they come to be part of FE today. In fact the term was reintroduced in 1995 as the Modern Apprenticeship; but now it meant something quite different. It was a competence-based qualification involving sponsorship by an employer and a regime of work-based training combined with the successful completion of a level 3 NVQ. In 2004, Young Apprenticeships were introduced for pupils still in compulsory education, enabling them to spend two days a week learning in the workplace. These, and similar arrangements, are now known simply as apprenticeships, the same title as was used pre-1983, but now describing a very different process.

In 1992, while colleges were still acclimatising themselves to the changes brought about by the 1986 act, the policy equivalent of an earthquake shook the entire sector and radically re-shaped it. *The Further and Higher Education Act*, approved by parliament in March of that year, put into motion the proposals that had been set out the previous year in the White Paper: *Education and Training for the 21st Century*. Colleges of Further Education were to be removed from local authority control and transformed into corporate bodies – businesses responsible for managing their own budgets – and funded indirectly by central government through newly created quangos (quasi-autonomous non-governmental organisations) or funding councils. This transformation in the operation and status of colleges became known as 'incorporation'. Teachers in colleges were now no longer employees of the local education authority but of the college itself, and this led to major changes in their conditions of service as college executives turned their attention to budgets and finance. In order to progress on the pay scale, teachers were now required to relinquish the long holidays, once the equivalent to those enjoyed by teachers in schools and to accept, in addition, longer working hours and often larger classes. Now operating outside the strategic control of local authorities and responsible for earning income, colleges were thrown into competition not only with one another but also with schools, since the *Further and Higher Education*

Act now allowed schools to introduce elements of vocational education into their sixth form provision. Colleges also had to compete with private training organisations who could now apply for government funding through the same funding councils. This entry into the world of competition and market forces was in line with a government policy informed by the belief that competition would bring about a raising of standards. According to this theory, poorly performing colleges would fail and close or be taken over by their stronger competitors. This ideology was the economic equivalent of Darwin's survival of the fittest, and it introduced a very different board game indeed.

Critical Thinking Activity 7

Here is Michael J. Sandel, Professor of Government at Harvard University, writing about markets:

The reach of markets, and market-oriented thinking, into aspects of life traditionally governed by nonmarket norms is one of the most significant developments of our time...[A] non-judgemental stance towards values lies at the heart of market reasoning and explains much of its appeal. But our reluctance to engage in moral and spiritual argument, together with our embrace of markets, has exacted a heavy price: it has drained public discourse of moral and civic energy, and contributed to the technocratic, managerial politics that affects many societies today.

(Sandel, 2013, pp 7, 14)

» *What is Sandel arguing here?*

» *How do you think he might apply this argument in the context of FE?*

Ch-ch-ch-changes

In subsequent decades there have been many more changes, as we know. The Foster Report of 2005 defined the purpose of FE categorically as the delivery of skills training. Funding bodies and regulatory bodies have come and gone in line with changes in government policy. We now have the Education and Training Foundation, known as the 'FE Guild' to oversee the sector and regulate standards. It is, of course, employer-led. But no subsequent changes have been quite so radical and far-reaching as those triggered by the 1992 act. And none have had such a resounding impact on defining the role and status of vocational education for the twenty-first century.

Chapter reflections

This chapter has set out to trace the origins of the Further Education sector and the factors that have shaped its role and status up to the present day. We've looked at themes that have remained constant across two centuries, such as assumptions about education, status and social class, as well as seeing how arguments about the purpose and curriculum for Further Education have changed over time. Using the analogy of a family tree, we have traced features of nineteenth-century vocational education that remain recognisable today, such as the idea that it is somehow less prestigious than a general or academic education. But we have also identified examples of where the family name has remained the same despite the legitimate line of descent being broken, as in the case of apprenticeships. And running parallel to vocational education we've also seen glimpses of another family tree: that of general or academic education, with its grammar schools, A levels and universities. At some points the branches of the two seem almost to touch, as with the provision of liberal education in the technical colleges of the mid-twentieth century and the introduction of vocational courses into schools in the 1990s. But, on the whole, the two lines of descent have remained separate over the two centuries we have explored here.

We've also used the image of a time-traveller, to highlight what has remained constant over the past 200 years and what has changed. The nineteenth-century tug of war about whether further education existed to serve the needs of the individual or the employer, for example, has continued; although our time-traveller will have seen it pulled back and forth, with a period in the mid-twentieth century when liberal education gained a temporary foothold before being well and truly trounced as a result of the 1992 act. Using these analogies we have been able to explore the origins of ideas about the value, status and purpose of further or vocational education, now known as Further Education, which might otherwise be accepted as inevitable and simply taken for granted. Our explorations have shown us how the rigid social structures and snobberies of the nineteenth century have cast a long shadow over our education and training system; but these investigations have also equipped us with the knowledge and understanding to challenge such outmoded ideas wherever we encounter them.

And finally, we have imagined the education and training system as a board game, so that we can stand back and more easily see the key factors which have contributed to the way Further Education is viewed today; factors such as selection, class and choice, and assumptions about the ultimate goals and 'gold standards' of education. In the chapters that follow we shall be looking again at some of these themes in relation to the more recent developments, and exploring ways they influence and inform our current experiences and practices.

Taking it further

If you would like to read further about education and social mobility you could look at:

Ball, S.J. (2008) *The Education Debate: Policy and Politics in the 21st Century*. London: Policy Press; and

Simon, B. (1999) *Education and the Social Order*. London: Lawrence and Wishart.

To find out more about the history of education and training up to the 1980s, you can read extracts from key policy documents in:

Maclure, J.S. (ed) (1986) *Educational Documents: England and Wales 1816 to the Present Day*. London: Methuen.

For insight into the 1980s debate about training schemes, you may enjoy the very lively argument in:

Finn, D. (1987) *Training Without Jobs*. Basingstoke: Macmillan.

For a full text version of the 1992 *Further and Higher Education Act* see www.legislation.gov.uk/ukpga/1992/13/contents

For further discussion of the 1944 *Education Act* (the Butler Act) and a full text download see www.educationengland.org.uk/history/chapter05.html

References

Finn, D. (1987) *Training Without Jobs*. Basingstoke: Macmillan.

Foster, A. (2005) *Realising the Potential: A Review of the Future Role of Further Education Colleges*. Annesley: DfES.

Maclure, J.S. (ed) (1986) *Educational Documents: England and Wales 1816 to the Present Day*. London: Methuen.

Sandel, M.J. (2013) *What Money Can't Buy: The Moral Limits of Markets*. London: Penguin Books.

3 Building status and dismantling the mutual damnation model

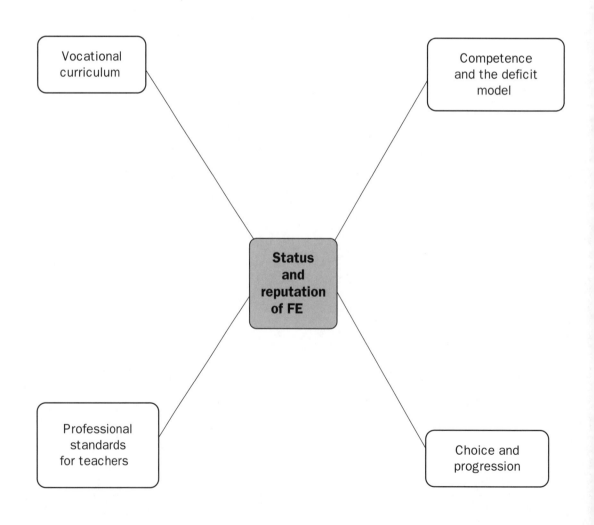

Vocational curriculum

Competence and the deficit model

Status and reputation of FE

Professional standards for teachers

Choice and progression

Chapter aims

This chapter is designed to help you explore:

- how the status of FE as 'second-best' is perpetuated and how this could be addressed;

- how the structure for vocational qualifications impacts on the role and self-image of teachers and learners;

- the relationship between education, training and employability;

- the debates around training and qualifications for teachers in FE.

What is the mutual damnation model?

Mutual damnation model sounds rather dramatic – and, in a way, it is. It's a sort of shorthand for a cyclical process of reputation damage in which FE provision finds itself trapped, where the sector becomes associated, in the public perception, with underachieving and disengaged learners. This, in turn, fosters the idea that vocational qualifications are for low achievers, so that consequently school students who are high achievers are advised against Further Education as a suitable progression route. This makes it more likely that some of those students who *are* guided towards FE will see it as a sort of failure on their part, a step in which they have had no choice; and so, seeing themselves in that sense as 'losers', they may lose any motivation to learn, become disengaged and fail to achieve. And there the cycle begins all over again.

Is this inevitable? That's one of the questions we're going to be exploring in this chapter. And, if we assume that it doesn't have to be this way, what can be done to break the mutual damnation cycle? We'll be considering to what extent the vocational qualifications framework itself may provide a way of addressing this problem and the part the sector-specific qualification for teachers may play in all of this. First, however, let's look at an example of how the mutual damnation model operates in practice.

CASE STUDY

Eloise's story

When I was at school, right, I wanted to be a teacher. I wanted to be a language teacher in a secondary school. My dad, he's Spanish, right. And I speak Spanish fluently as well as English. So what I wanted was to go to university and get a qualification as a teacher teaching Spanish in an English school. But what they said to me in Year 11, right, was that I wasn't going to be able to stay on at school to take A levels because my grades weren't good enough. But I needed A levels to go to uni. But what they said was, You can't come into the sixth form with those grades. So why don't you go to college and do a childcare course? It's a bit like teaching. It's a bit like what you want to do. *Well, I only didn't get good grades because I'd been not working hard enough, right. Going out and that. I wish now I'd done more work. It wasn't that I'm stupid or anything. If they'd given me a chance I'd've showed them. But anyway, they wouldn't let me stay on, so I went on the childcare course at college.*

What else was I going to do? I mean, there wasn't any other option was there? But I didn't want to do childcare. I'm not interested in little kids. I don't want to work with little kids. Ever. So it was pointless really. But there wasn't any other course at the college I wanted to do either. What I wanted to do was stay on in the sixth form, do A levels and go to university, right. So I was bored. And I was pissed off. And mostly I didn't turn up for lessons. Mostly I hung about on the bridge, having a laugh and a drink with some other people who didn't like being at college. And one day our neighbour, Sheena – my mum's friend – saw me there and she looked disgusted. And she told my mum, right. And then I was in big trouble. And mum says to me that Sheena's daughter wants to work with young kids and wants to do a course in childcare. But, after seeing me, Sheena won't let her apply to the college because now she thinks the childcare course there is for losers – that's her opinion of me, a loser! – and she thinks the students there'll be a bad influence. So her daughter's going to stay on at school instead and do A levels. And she'll be able to do that, because her grades are OK. So how stupid is that? There's me on the course and I don't want to be; and there's her, right, not allowed on the course just because some of us are showing how pissed off we are about not being given any choice about our future.

Once we've heard from Eloise about her disappointingly low achievement at school, we can break down her story into six stages:

- FE seen as a sector for low achievers, leading to...

- her reluctant entry onto a course that holds no interest for her, leading to...

- her lack of motivation and engagement, leading to...

- her disaffected behaviour, leading to...

- her attitude being taken as representative of FE learners as a whole, leading to...

- FE being seen as a sector for low achievers.

We can see from this how the story comes full circle. As long as there is an assumption that FE is predominantly for those learners who do not achieve highly in school, whether they want to go into FE or not, that state of affairs will become self-perpetuating. This is what is meant by the mutual damnation model. In some ways this is a different issue from the historical prejudices about work and status that we discussed in Chapter 2. It's much more to do with the lack of alternative options for some school leavers and their frustiation to do with their aspirations. Many learners, perhaps the majority, enter FE by choice, to learn skills that they hope will enable them to work in the vocational area where their ambition and interest lies. But it's nevertheless certainly the case that some are at college *not* by choice, but primarily because they didn't do well at school; and this is where the heart of the problem seems to lie. Research supports this view. For example, Fuller and Macfadyen (2012) argue from their research that it is largely pupils with good grades who are encouraged to stay on at school. We perhaps shouldn't be surprised, given that market competition has operated in education since the 1990s, that it is the schools, not the students, who have the final choice over who will stay on after the age of 16. And, as Swift and Fisher (2012) point out in their research paper, the need to meet performance targets means that schools will obviously wish to retain pupils at 16 on the basis of their academic achievement. Swift and Fisher also point to *the ambivalent status surrounding vocational education* (2012, p 207) as some-thing that may not only deter more ambitious students from opting for FE at 16, but may also have a detrimental effect on levels of motivation and engagement in young people for whom it is the only option – which was exactly what we saw in Eloise's case.

Alison Wolf, in her book *Does Education Matter?* (2002, p 56), describes the FE sector, with irony, as a provision *for other people's children*, highlighting that commonly held notion that it is somehow a second-best option. Research by Baird *et al* (2012) supports this idea, sug-gesting that learners in FE tend to express lower aspirations than learners who stay on in schools. Of course, we could argue, after listening to Eloise's story, that these learners may well have *had* high aspirations, but – finding themselves in FE – feel compelled to abandon them. We know that there is no reason necessarily for them to do this, of course. FE offers a parallel, alternative route into higher education, through vocational qualifications, general qualifications or access courses. But school leavers don't automatically know this. If college is presented to them only in terms of a vocational course they've no particular interest in, they may well ditch their previously held ambitions and just give up. This would suggest, of course, that there is a need for clearer, personalised progression advice and guidance before the key point of transition.

Critical Thinking Activity 1

» *You'll notice that in this chapter research is cited in order to support the arguments and the points being made. If you look at the References section at the end of this chapter you'll find that all the authors and researchers who are cited by name here are listed there in alphabetical order, along with the title of their work that's been referred to and – for research papers – the name and edition of the journal it is published in. Some of these academic journals are available to access online through your college or university library. So you can read the full text if you would like to find out more about what these researchers have to say and how they went about collecting their data. You may find it useful to note, for when you are required to produce your own academic writing or assignments:*

  the form in which these references appear in the text: author/s surname and date;

  the need to cite a page number for all direct quotes;

  the abbreviation et al *used within the text for multi-authored work, with the names listed in full in the final References.*

» *Returning to Eloise's story, you probably noticed that there were several opportunities where the mutual damnation cycle could have been broken. Make a note of where these opportunities arose, what interventions could have been made and who, in each instance, could have made them. Consider particularly how any of Eloise's FE teachers might have been able to make a difference. What could they have done? And what reasons might there be for them not having done so?*

The vocational qualification framework

Some have argued that another factor in this cycle of poor achievement, lost ambition and low esteem may be the very nature of the vocational curriculum itself. 'Vocational' is an interesting word, as we saw in Chapter 1. It means more than just 'work' or 'job' because in some contexts, such as medicine, we take it to imply both a special calling and a professional dedication. So, is the discrepancy in status between doctors and, say, hairdressers simply about potential earning power; or is it that the work of doctors (and lawyers and clergy and similar professionals) is not linked to nineteenth- and twentieth-century ideas of industry and commerce? Or perhaps it's that the training for these professions draws on a body of knowledge that is relatively independent of socio-economic systems and not easily reducible to a set of competences.

The vocational curriculum in its FE context, on the other hand, has been described as both repetitious and instrumental, particularly when based on a set of competences. In her *Review of Vocational Education* (2011) – also known as the Wolf Report – Alison Wolf suggests that this emphasis on 'competence' may encourage young learners to regard the process of learning simply as a tick list of things they 'can do'. The disadvantage of this is that it fails to engage their enthusiasm for deeper levels of understanding or for the process of learning itself. This is not a new argument. As long ago as 1995, Reeves was arguing that this sort of instrumental curriculum encourages in learners a *tacit acceptance that proper education is rewarded with accreditation not by gratification* (1995, p 105). This argument is worth looking at more closely. After all, why should we need 'gratification' – that is, pleasure and satisfaction in what we're doing – if all we're in college for is to get the accreditation? Having accreditation as the sole goal is what we mean when we talk about instrumental education or training; where the learning itself is regarded as just a means to an end, rather than as a process which we also enjoy for its own sake. More than a century ago, the designer and writer, William Morris (1834–96) was condemning what he called *useless toil*, which he defined as work that held no *hope of pleasure in our daily creative skill* (Morris, 1888, p 4). This is what Wolf and Reeves may be getting at here: that unless learners are encouraged to find enjoyment or satisfaction in the day-to-day processes of learning, the potential we have to raise their levels of motivation is drastically reduced. And this may be particularly so in the current economic climate, where learners are all too aware that even success in gaining competence-based accreditation won't guarantee them success in the job market. As Wolf (2011) points out, learners in FE are well aware of the low value often attached to the qualifications for which they are being urged to work; and so, if neither the learning itself nor the final accreditation hold out any real promise of satisfaction, it isn't surprising that levels of motivation are sometimes very low.

We know that since the Foster Report of 2005, the purpose of the sector has been identified as being primarily one of skills training. The skills training curriculum itself may, suggests Bathmaker (2005), compromise the sector's position and status in what we are increasingly coming to recognise as a *knowledge society*. In a knowledge economy the concept of 'observable skills' and 'competence' become, to some extent, devalued. So it may be that this aspect of its curriculum, too, helps to explain why FE is currently regarded by many as a progression route for those who have failed at school.

Critical Thinking Activity 2

This section has explored a number of arguments that suggest that the disengagement of some young learners in FE may be partly due to the current format and content of the vocational curriculum itself. These arguments can be summarised as follows:

a)   The assessment-led nature of the curriculum can mean the learner experiences it as repetitious and instrumental, rather than interesting and challenging.

b)   The emphasis on outcomes – in the form of competence and accreditation – leads learners to undervalue the process or experience of learning.

c)   Awareness that the qualifications they are working towards, although 'vocational', do not guarantee employment undermines learners' motivation.

»   Which of these arguments, if any, do you find the most compelling?

»   If you were asked to design an ideal curriculum for young learners in your vocational area, what would it look like?

»   How would it address the problems we've been discussing in this section of the chapter?

You might find it useful to explain and discuss your ideas with a colleague or mentor.

Does a vocational curriculum necessarily have to be instrumental?

The short answer to this question is: well, yes, to some extent; because by definition its aim is to equip and qualify learners for joining the workforce. But it's by no means inevitable that it should be entirely driven by the assessment of observable competences and understanding. The National Vocational Qualification (NVQ) model that dominates the vocational curriculum today is relatively new in historical terms. As we saw in Chapter 2, this was introduced in 1986 as part of a government-driven initiative to rationalise existing disparate vocational qualifications within one coherent framework. The argument for this was that the existing situation, with various bodies awarding qualifications at levels defined by themselves, made it very difficult to pin down what individual qualifications meant, in terms of standards of attainment and equivalence with others. The NVQ system, its standards and competencies informed by the expressed needs of employers, was designed to address this problem. The term *competence* replaced *learning outcome* or *learning objective* and, for the teacher, the emphasis moved from teaching or supporting learning to assessing learning. In theory, anyone who could demonstrate the relevant competences to a qualified assessor could be accredited with a qualification or a unit of a qualification without necessarily attending a course of study. In their new role as 'assessors', teachers in FE – however skilled or experienced – were required to gain an NVQ unit known as the Assessor Award to demonstrate that they themselves were 'competent' to assess. This did not always go down too well.

It seems that there was originally some intention that NVQs would provide a route not only to employment but also into higher education. In 1991 the government White Paper *Education and Training for the Twenty-first Century* claimed that there would be a clear equivalence between NVQs and general academic qualifications at the corresponding level. At that time this would mean that a level 2 NVQ would be equivalent to four or five good GCSEs, and a level 3 NVQ would be equivalent to two A levels. The word 'equivalence' is a slippery one, of course. Was this saying that learners on each of these routes would acquire skills and knowledge at the same level; or that the two types of qualification would have equal currency for the purposes of progression, either into work or into higher education? Or did it imply that both routes, the vocational and the academic, would be accorded equal esteem in the eyes of the public and particularly of employers? As it turned out, none of these proved to be the case in any meaningful or general sense. NVQs were not accepted as an entry qualification by universities (although their distant cousin, the GNVQ, sometimes was, by some); and it seems that employers continued, on the whole, to favour job applicants who had GCSEs in English and mathematics. The failure to establish a general acceptance of equivalence was perhaps in part due to the fact that NVQs were seen to require comparatively little written reportage, despite efforts to emphasise the component element of underpinning knowledge. There is also a problem inherent within the competent/not competent model of assessment decision, which is that there is little incentive for the potentially excellent performer to excel. They will still achieve the outcome of 'competent', just as the less hardworking learner will who scrapes through, but only just. This once again raises the issue of motivation in relation to the vocational curriculum.

So, did the introduction of competence-based training achieve what it set out to do? In some ways, yes, because it brought about a rationalisation of vocational qualifications and introduced a framework which provided a national standardisation of levels. It also fulfilled its aim of creating a curriculum that was employer-led. Performance criteria were drawn up by lead bodies that were made up largely of employer representatives from the relevant vocational area. The aim here was to provide employers with the sort of workforce they wanted in order to support the economy. However, the seismic shift from an input-driven to an assessment-driven curriculum model may also have brought its disadvantages, according to the arguments we have discussed in this chapter so far. Certainly it might be claimed that its instrumental emphasis on skills and outcomes, rather than on learning and process, contributed to creating a wider divide between the vocational and the general (or academic) curriculum, rather than bringing them closer together.

Critical Thinking Activity 3

This section has looked at some of the ideas behind the introduction of a competence-based curriculum. Drawing on what you have read so far, and your own experiences of teaching and learning, consider how you would answer the following questions:

» *What are the advantages of an instrumental, competence-based curriculum for the learner?*

» *What are the advantages for the teacher/assessor?*

» *And what are the advantages for the employer?*

» *What might be the disadvantages of this model for the teacher/assessor?*

» *What types of learning might be excluded by such a model, and does this matter?*

» *Are there disadvantages for the learner? If so, what do you consider these might be?*

» *And finally, the employer. Might there be disadvantages as well as advantages to the employer in having employees who have acquired their skills and knowledge through a competence-based curriculum? What might these be?*

You may find it useful to discuss some or all of these questions with a colleague or mentor.

Education, training and employability

Now we get to the million dollar question: should anyone's education or training be entirely focused on competency in preparation for work, even in the context of the vocational curriculum? Does such an approach, as Reeves (1995, p 103) once argued, tend to alienate learners because all it's doing is simply reflecting *the tedium of the work routine*? If the sector is regarded purely as a means for equipping learners with the specific competences they need for a particular vocational area – for making them employable – it could be argued that it is predicated from the outset on a deficit model of the learner. That is, that the learner is lacking something – is deficient in some way – which the vocational curriculum will supply. Further, and more widely, it suggests that anyone who cannot find employment must also be deficient, and that this deficiency can be cured by the individual entering into a course of skills training. This implicit explanation of unemployment – that it's caused by a deficit of skills in those who are unemployed – is what, in a detective story, we would call a 'red herring'. It draws our attention away from the primary causes of mass unemployment, which are economic ones. And it takes as its starting point what the learner lacks, not what they already have – their potential.

Nevertheless, a skilled workforce is obviously a necessity, and we have certainly come increasingly to think of learning in terms of employability and meeting the needs of the economy. But does this sort of language cause us to leave out something important when we're talking and thinking about young people and their learning? For example, what of the talents or interests that are part of what makes that learner who they are? Should there be room in the curriculum to encourage and develop these alongside a set of vocational competences? And what about the periods of unemployment that many will face in the current economy? What skills, resources or interests are we giving young people to fall back on when they are not in paid work? And what about their friendships and family life that for most of them will be central to their wellbeing in their future life – as much or more so as their jobs and career? Should there be room in the curriculum for learning about empathy, negotiation, listening skills? About developing a moral compass? About social responsibility or money management?

When we ponder whether there is a distinction to be made between education and training, we may arrive at an answer that puts all those kinds of 'skills for life' into the category of education, and defines training as being just about vocational competences. What we need to remember, however, is that the sector we are concerned with is known as Further *Education*; and that despite all the name changes, its central concern must always be with the learners and the quality of their learning experience.

Critical Thinking Activity 4

» *Reflecting on what has been said in this chapter so far, think about the wider curriculum in your own college. What types of provision lie outside that aimed at specific vocational areas? For example, does the college offer adult basic skills or A levels? In what sense might these also be considered to be part of a vocational curriculum?*

» *Read the following passage from a research paper by Halliday written more than a decade ago. To what extent is the argument he is making still relevant today? And how does this argument contribute to our discussion of the mutual damnation model?*

It is undoubtedly the case...that those who can acquire qualifications with only little extrinsic value are very unlikely to be able to exchange them to realize something that is intrinsically worthwhile...It is also therefore futile for Colleges of FE to concentrate their efforts on helping the maximum number of individuals to acquire the maximum number of so-called competencies as if the exchange value of those competencies were all that mattered and as if their exchange value was high.

(Halliday, 1999, p 55)

Teacher, trainer, instructor, assessor?

Before the introduction of the Further Education National Training Organisation (FENTO) standards in 1999, a teaching qualification for teachers in FE was not mandatory. In 2005, FENTO was replaced by Lifelong Learning UK (LLUK) whose Standards and Verification unit, known as SVUK, had the role of endorsing and policing the updated LLUK standards. Both LLUK and SVUK have now disappeared into the dustbin of history; but at the date of publication, standards are still in place and teachers in FE are obliged to demonstrate that they meet them. No bad thing, surely? Well, as a matter of fact, opinion is divided on this matter. Two main arguments are levelled against the standards. One is about the reasoning behind them being introduced in the first place; and the other is about the fact that their format looks very like a set of competences.

In 1998 the then Secretary of State for Education, David Blunkett, addressed the Association of Colleges annual conference and announced the setting up of a 'Standards Fund' aimed at raising standards of achievement in FE. It was targeted specifically at improving standards of teaching and updating teachers' skills in their specialist area. There was, said Blunkett, *too much poor or inadequate teaching* in the sector (1998, p 2). The development and introduction of the original national standards for FE teachers was aimed at addressing this problem. We have seen the deficit model of the learner, and here, claim some, we have the deficit model of the teacher. Although the introduction of standards is clearly a sensible and reasonable policy in itself, what critics have objected to is the implication that standards of achievement in FE could be raised solely by addressing the performance of teachers. What this suggests, they argue, is that low achievement is always the result of poor teaching, rather than of other, wider, endemic factors such as those we've been considering in this chapter: lack of choice; lack of employment prospects; uninspiring curriculum, and so on. By emphasising teaching standards, policymakers are able to make the wider causes of learner disengagement disappear from the discourses about motivation and achievement.

Then there's the second line of argument, which is about the form the FE teaching qualification takes. Lucas (2007), for example, argues that having teacher training for the sector that is based on 'standards' rather than on 'knowledge' fails to take account of the complexities that the learning process involves, particularly in regard to motivation. It places too much emphasis, Lucas claims, on the concept of vocational education and work-based learning as simply a process of learning by doing; and this has the effect of lowering its status and value. The instrumental nature of the current standards framework, which itself looks very much like a set of competences, could be seen as undermining FE teachers' sense of self-esteem, self-efficacy and professionalism. Most teachers, argue Robson et al (2004) understand 'professionalism' as being about the ability and the willingness to extend their practice beyond the curriculum requirements. This might, for example, include the teacher discovering ways to increase their theoretical understanding of how best to engage and motivate their learners, or how to build more constructive relationships with them. What this argument is saying is that the competence format of the standards makes them both descriptive and prescriptive. That is, they emphasise *what* teachers should do rather than *why* they should do it that way; and they exclude some areas of skills and understanding that would enhance teachers' concept of themselves as professionals. The instrumental nature of the standards excludes, for example, the approach to teaching that Knowles (1984) refers to as *andragogy* (the education of adults, as opposed to pedagogy – the education of children) in which the role of the teacher is to support learning rather than to instruct, and where the teacher–learner relationship is less hierarchical and more mutually enriching. Nor does it accommodate Paulo Freire's idea of learning as a process of transformation and empowerment (Freire, 1996).

Critics of the existing standards point out that these embody two discourses or claims about FE that have never been substantiated. One is that deficiencies in teaching are the main cause of learners' low achievement. The other is that instrumental, competence-based training is the most effective approach at all levels, from school leavers enrolled for a basic level NVQ to the teaching staff whose role is to instruct and assess them.

Critical Thinking Activity 5

We've looked at two arguments here: one that questions whether some learners' lack of engagement and achievement in FE is simply the result of poor teaching; and one suggesting that teaching standards that look like competences are unnecessarily prescriptive in that they narrow our understanding of the teacher's role and limit the range of teachers' professional practice.

» *What is your own response to these arguments? Do you find them convincing?*

» *Whether you agree with them or not, consider how you might construct a counter-argument, justifying competence-based standards for FE teachers.*

» *Teacher, lecturer, trainer, instructor, or assessor? How do you think of your own role? Does it matter what we call ourselves, or does 'teacher', for example, imply something different from 'instructor'? (You might like to look back here to Chapter 1, Critical Thinking Activity 1.)*

» *What bearing do the arguments we've looked at in this section have on the identity and role of the FE teacher?*

Superteacher or masterchef?

Unlike schools, where teachers usually come directly from higher education to begin their teaching career, one of the key characteristics of FE is that many of its teachers have come into the sector from a previous career in the world of work in order to pass on their knowledge, craft or skills to a new generation. The internal organisation of colleges, therefore, can seem quite tribal to an outsider. Construction, hairdressing, business studies, electronics, sports and leisure management, and so on; most of the teachers in each of these departments or schools come into the FE teaching profession first and foremost as professionals in another line of work entirely. Their sense of themselves as teachers first, electricians or beauty therapists second is something that has to develop over time. You may be in the process of this changeover yourself. So what is it that turns you into a teacher, that makes 'teacher' part of your identity? Is it adherence to the professional standards, or is it something else? Here is one teacher's view. You may like to compare his experience with your own.

CASE STUDY

Marlon's story

My name's Marlon and I joined this college's School of Hospitality and Catering about two years ago. Before that I'd been working as a chef in various hotels. My last one was the X Hotel over on the coast. I was involved in training some of the lads in the kitchen and I'd done my trainers award, so when this job came up I thought, Why not? The hours fit in much better with family life. My kids are starting to remember who I am now! But do I enjoy it as much? I'm not sure. Some of the learners we get in here – I'm not sure why they're here. They're just not interested. And would you trust some of them with a big knife? [Laughs] I try talking to them, you know: What do you want out of this course? That sort of thing. But they're never going to get a job in a kitchen. It's not what they want to do. And I go home some nights thinking, you know, why bother? But then you get a good day – you get a learner or a bunch of them who up until that point had been a complete pain, and suddenly, you know, they've got it! And you can see them thinking, Hey! I can do this! And it's an amazing feeling, that. To have made a difference to someone. And you know they're going to make it, they've found something they enjoy and they're going to be good at. And they've found out it's creative and satisfying and all those things. You see them taking a pride in it and knowing something about themselves they didn't know before. Those are the days I feel like a real teacher. Other days, though, I still think of myself first and foremost as a chef. A chef first and a teacher second. Yes, I did the course and got my FE teaching qualification. I did that the first year I was here, the professional standards and all that. But that's not what makes me feel like a teacher. It's when I get through to these kids and I make a difference. For me, that's what being a teacher's really about.

Chapter reflections

In this chapter we have examined some of the reasons why the FE sector is sometimes regarded as a route for learners who haven't achieved well at school, and how this assumption is perpetuated. We've looked specifically at some of the arguments that researchers and academics have put forward about this, and how these should be referenced if you are producing a piece of academic writing. The issues explored in this chapter can be summarised as follows:

» *The cyclical process of reputation damage that operates as a mutual damnation model where pupils with good grades are encouraged to stay on at school rather than progress to college and the detrimental effect this has on the motivation of young people for whom FE is the only option.*

» *Whether FE teachers are able to do anything to break this cycle.*

» *The argument that the nature of the vocational curriculum itself contributes to learner disengagement.*

» *The impact of competence-based NVQs on teachers and learners.*

» *The link between competences and a deficit model of the learner.*

» *The argument that the instrumental nature of the professional standards for FE teachers restricts the teacher's role and contributes to the idea of FE as a second-best choice.*

Taking it further

If you would like to learn more about any of the arguments presented in this chapter you could read any one of the works referenced below. The papers by Fuller and Macfadyen (2012) and by Baird *et al* (2012) are particularly interesting and very straightforward to read. If you present the full reference, you should be able to access a copy through your library.

References

Baird, J., Rose, J. and McWhirter, A. (2012) So Tell Me What You Want: A Comparison of FE College and Other Post-16 Students' Aspirations. *Research in Post-Compulsory Education*, 17(3): 293–310.

Bathmaker, A. (2005) Hanging in or Shaping a Future: Defining a Role for Vocationally Related Learning in a 'Knowledge' Society. *Journal of Education Policy*, 20(1): 81–100.

Blunkett, D. (1998) Speech to AoC annual conference, reported in FEDA editorial, *Reform*, 1999, 2.

Freire, P. (1996) *The Pedagogy of the Oppressed*. London: Penguin Education.

Fuller, C. and Macfadyen, T. (2012) 'What, with your Grades?' Students' Motivations and Experiences of Vocational Courses in Further Education. *Journal of Vocational Education and Training*, 64(1): 87–101.

Halliday, J. (1999) Qualifications in FE: Inclusion and Exchange. *Journal of Further and Higher Education*, 23: 53–60.

Knowles, M. (1984) *Androgogy in Action: Applying Modern Principles of Adult Learning*. US: Jossey-Bass.

Lucas, N. (2007) Rethinking Initial Teacher Education for Further Education Teachers: From a Standards-led to a Knowledge-based Approach. *Teacher Education*, 18(2): 93–106.

Morris, W. (1888/2008) *Useful Work Versus Useless Toil*. London: Penguin.

Reeves, F. (1995) *The Modernity of Further Education*. Bilston and Ticknall: Bilston College Publications.

Robson, J., Bailey, B. and Larkin, S. (2004) Adding Value: Investigating the Discourse of Professionalism Adopted by Vocational Teachers in Further Education Colleges. *Journal of Education and Work*, 17(2): 183–95.

Swift, J. and Fisher, R. (2012) Choosing Vocational Education: Some Views from Young People in West Yorkshire. *Research in Post-Compulsory Education*, 17(2): 207–21.

Wolf, A. (2002) *Does Education Matter? Myths About Education and Economic Growth*. London: Penguin.

Wolf, A. (2011) *Review of Vocational Education [The Wolf Report]*. London: Department for Education.

4 Ladders, weddings and machinery: reading the White Papers

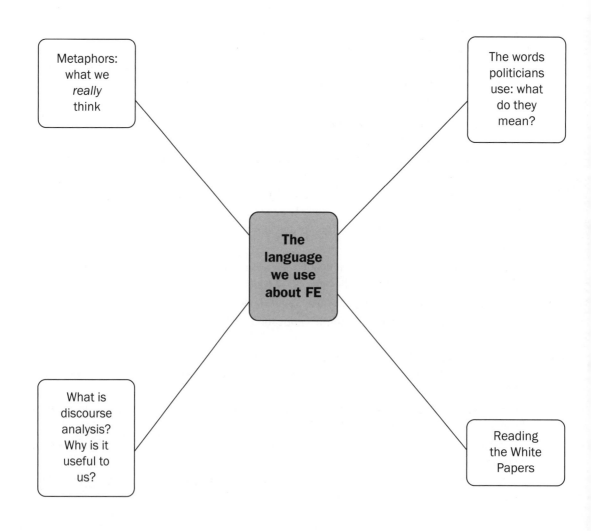

Metaphors: what we *really* think

The words politicians use: what do they mean?

The language we use about FE

What is discourse analysis? Why is it useful to us?

Reading the White Papers

Chapter aims

This chapter is designed to help you gain an understanding of:

*   successive governments' policies for the sector, and the discourse about 'parity of esteem';

*   the role language can play in either reinforcing or challenging preconceived ideas about the FE sector.

Introduction

In Chapter 2 we looked at the origins of the FE system and saw how these continue to shape the way people think about the sector. In this chapter we're going to explore the evidence for this that can be found in the language of policy documents such as government White Papers. We're going to see how a careful choice of words can be used to reinforce key policy ideas. We'll consider, too, how the metaphors and other imagery employed in such documents sometimes demonstrate a preconception about the purpose and status of FE; a preconception that contradicts those surface claims being made about parity of esteem for the sector, its qualifications, its teachers and its learners. Although this is a serious topic, it can have its light-hearted side as we'll see in the unintentional humour that results from some of these language games. We shall also be looking at the language we and other professionals use when talking about the sector, and what it can tell us about our own underlying attitudes and assumptions.

The language of the White Papers

In this section we're going to look at some of the late twentieth-century landmark White Papers that set out the policy for the major reforms to FE that have shaped the sector we know today. We're going to look specifically at how the language in them has been used to reinforce the ideas and beliefs that underlie the policies and so make their 'argument' more convincing. The word 'argument' is a problematic one here because the purpose of White Papers is to set out and justify government policy. They tend, therefore, to rely not so much on argument as on persuasion. The distinction is an important one. An argument rests on evidence, as you've seen in other chapters of this book where specific research or other named sources are cited to support the point being made. And where there is an argument, there is always a counter-argument, and this should be acknowledged and addressed. In White Papers this is not normally the case. Because their purpose is to persuade, they rely heavily on the power of language – what we call rhetoric – to win us over. This is one of the things that makes them so interesting to analyse in retrospect, because we can see values and attitudes being encouraged and developing over time until they are masquerading as common sense or 'truth' or 'the way things really are'. Some of these landmark White Papers will already be familiar. Several have already been cited in Chapters 2 and 3 as part of the story of how FE has developed over the decades. But now our attention turns from *what* they said to *how* they said it, and the way this continues to influence the thinking about FE, ours as well as the policymakers'.

Here come the skills: *A New Training Initiative*, 1981

The full title of this White Paper was *A New Training Initiative: A Programme for Action*. As we've already seen, it changed the face of FE by reforming the apprenticeship system into one that was based on competences achieved rather than time served, establishing training programmes for adults wishing to update or acquire skills and introducing the Youth Training Scheme (YTS). There are keywords in this document that are repeated over and over. One of these is *skills*. An idea central to the paper is that a more highly skilled workforce will mean more jobs and a stronger economy. Sometimes this idea is expressed slightly differently: that there are few jobs for school leavers but that there will be more if these school leavers have some work-related training. On page 9 of the original document there is a categoric 'promise' that the YTS will be a training *which improves [young people's] prospects of employment*. This cluster of arguments is an interesting one because it still persists today, despite several decades of contrary experience. That a more highly skilled workforce increases economic strength can now be viewed with some scepticism from the viewpoint of a world recession. The argument for continued wide-scale training in specific skills or competences has been accepted readily and uncritically as part of our common-sense understanding. This diverts us, however from what would otherwise be two obvious questions: why the emphasis on training when there are increasingly fewer jobs? And will skills training for school leavers really *create* jobs for school leavers? It might be more logical to argue that training school leavers will create jobs for trainers! Another problem with these arguments is that they present a deficit model of the school leaver that goes like this: because they lack skills, there are no jobs for them; and because there are no jobs, the economy is not flourishing. Therefore the problem with the economy is the fault of unskilled school leavers. From our position several decades on, this looks like a pretty weak argument!

And why does the school leaver lack skills? Well, inevitably the implication is that it's the fault of the schools. The White Paper tells us that we must have *better preparation for working life in full time education* (p 2) and *better vocational preparation in schools* (p 10); that employer links with schools will *help pupils <u>and teachers</u> to gain a closer understanding of the...economic base of our society* (p 5, my emphasis). So here the argument goes a step further and suggests that the deficit in school leavers' skills is due to a deficiency in schools and of teachers. So is it teachers who are ultimately responsible for the weakness of the economy? This White Paper certainly leaves us thinking so, and it played a large part in what Stephen Ball (1990) refers to as the *discourse of derision* directed at teachers from this time onwards. As well as implying that employers can teach them a thing or two, another way in which this White Paper puts teachers in their place is to always put them at or near the last place in any list of stakeholders. For example, *employers, unions, education and training bodies* (p 3); *representatives of industry and education* (p 6); *employers, employees, unions, educationists and Government* (p 14) – perhaps only grammar or good manners saving them from last place here! The only list in which teachers come first is one in which expenses are being itemised: *the main items being teachers' and instructors' salaries, buildings and equipment* (p 13). It is unlikely that the word order in any of these lists is accidental. After all, the function of White Papers is to persuade the public that the government's view is the correct one, and so attention will have been given to the likely impact of the rank order in lists such as these.

As well as *skills*, we also find the words *standards* and *competence* frequently used in this document, sometimes combined as *standards of competence*, a term that was to become central to subsequent developments in vocational education. Twice in this White Paper its proposals are referred to as *proper training*, implying a blanket criticism of all existing and previous training provision including, presumably, the well-respected original apprenticeship model. That phrase '*proper* training' may remind us of the '*useful* knowledge' advocated by nineteenth-century politicians, as we saw in Chapter 2. Both raise the same questions: 'proper' or 'useful' to whom? In both cases the answer seems to be: employers.

One of the most interesting aspects of this White Paper, however, is where it signals the beginnings of government thinking about 'general vocational' provision for students aged 17+ in schools and colleges. This is what it says:

> This will be designed particularly for those with modest examination achievements at 16+ who are not looking towards higher education.
>
> (DoE, 1981, p 5, para 16)

By the time this provision arrived, in the form of GNVQs, claims were being made by ministers that this was to be an alternative route to higher education, different from A levels but equal, and having parity of esteem. And indeed, some students did use their GNVQ qualification to gain access to university. But a careful reading of *A New Training Initiative* shows clearly that this was not what politicians originally had in mind. Rather, the general vocational route was to be for lower achievers – those with 'modest' results in their GCSEs – a concept of general vocational education that governments, ironically, were to spend the following 30 years denying.

Standards and competence:
Working Together – Education and Training, 1986

The next key White Paper followed five years later and was again pivotal, in that it introduced NVQs. The exhortation that we should be 'working together' is given weight by its opening paragraph that, like all good rallying cries, identifies for us an external threat against which to unite. We live, this White Paper tells us, *in a world of determined, educated, trained and strongly motivated competitors* (DES, 1986, para 1.1) and these are threatening our *survival* (para 1.2). The emphasis on *skills, standards, competence* and *standards of competence* continues in this document, while at the same time a new set of words make an appearance; words that were to become increasingly familiar in subsequent policy documents: *choice, quality, partnership* and *relevant*. But *needs* is perhaps the most frequent key word in the *Working Together* White Paper; not the needs of learners, but the needs of the labour market; the needs of the modern world; and the needs of employers. Blame for the UK's poor showing in qualifications and training is apportioned two ways. First of all, claims the paper, it's partly the fault of the population in general having the wrong *attitudes* and failing so far to *acquire the desire to learn* (DES, 1986, para 1.4). And it's also the fault of the teaching profession, which is why it is necessary *to raise teaching quality and teacher motivation*. However, no attempt is made in the paper to construct an argument or explanation either for the population of (allegedly) reluctant learners, or for the (alleged) lack of motivation in teachers. We might think there would be sense in asking why are people reluctant to learn and why are teachers poorly motivated before proposing solutions to the problem. When key issues are left unexplored like this, it is an indication of rhetoric at work. You wouldn't be likely to get away with that in a piece of written coursework. And this is why citing or quoting White Papers uncritically – in other words, taking their unsubstantiated claims to be reasoned arguments – is not good academic practice. They are written to persuade; and, as an educational professional working within a democratic system, it is part of your responsibility to consider them with a critical eye from the perspective of your professional experience.

Critical Thinking Activity 1

» On the Department of Education website www.education.gov.uk you will find a 'wordcloud' summary of the 2013 Schools White Paper, The Importance of Teaching. What does it tell you about the main themes of this recent document? Do these also reflect any of the current issues in FE? Are there any echoes of the key words found in the papers from the1980s that we've been just been discussing? If so, what conclusions do you draw from this, three decades on?

» Using the search term 'Tech Bacc' conduct an internet search to find out more about the arguments surrounding the proposal to introduce the Technological Baccalaurate in 2013. Look particularly at the key words used in the government argument. Do you see anything familiar here? Anything new?

All change! *Education and Training for the 21st Century*, 1991

A decade on from *A New Training Initiative*, another White Paper, *Education and Training for the 21st Century*, brought further upheavals to FE. It's a document that crops up several times in this book because the changes it introduced radically changed the way FE was to operate. As we saw in Chapter 2, it removed FE colleges from local authority control so that they took on the status of corporate bodies, changing the terms of employment for its teachers. It also introduced AS levels in schools, and the GNVQs, an idea presented in broad terms in the 1986 White Paper as a provision for less able students, but now heralded as a route having *parity of esteem* with A levels. Indeed, *parity of esteem* is a recurring phrase in this document. We saw in Chapter 2 how this claim has proved in the past to be wildly overoptimistic. It's important to notice that, at the time the claim was first being made, no student had yet completed a GNVQ. No one had tried to use it to enter higher education, nor to gain employment. Its value as a currency for progression was completely unknown. On what grounds, then, could a claim about parity be justified? Parity – equal worth in the eyes of the world – cannot be achieved simply by government ministers saying it is so. This is rhetoric at work again; and perhaps you have noticed it at work again since, in the introduction of foundation degrees ten years later in 2001, for example; or the ministerial argument for introducing the Tech Bacc in 2013. In this 1991 White Paper the claim is made over and over, and expressed in a number of ways: *Equality of status* (DES, 1991, para 1.2); *equal esteem* (para 1.5); *equally valued* (para 3.1), and so on. But this assertion is never developed in terms of how this might be achieved, or what obstacles might lie in the way. The most that is said is that the government _want_ equal esteem for vocational qualifications, and that these _deserve_ *equal recognition* (p 24, my emphasis). The use of repetition in place of reasoned argument is another characteristic of rhetoric.

Choice is another frequently used word in this 1991 document. We have already seen in Chapter 3 how choice became increasingly the prerogative of schools, employers and higher education, leaving some groups of learners with little or no choice at all over their progression route at 16. But here we are told that learners' freedom of choice will reliably result from the government policy set out in this paper. *Collins English Dictionary* gives two definitions of rhetoric that are well illustrated in this policy document. Rhetoric is, says the dictionary: *the art of using [language] to persuade or influence*; and *discourse that pretends to significance but lacks true meaning*. In paragraph 10.1 of the 1991 White Paper we can see both of these at work in one carefully worded sentence:

> They [the government plans set out in the paper] will create better opportunities for young people from all backgrounds, of both sexes, from inner cities and elsewhere.

The cleverness of this wording (despite the fact that it is another unsubstantiated claim) lies in its occupation of the high moral ground. It manoeuvres the reader into a position where to argue against these government plans looks tantamount to aligning oneself with racists, sexists and snobs!

Choice and competitiveness: White Papers 1992–95

By the next landmark White Paper, the word *choice* has become so dominant that it now forms part of the title. *Choice and Diversity* (DES, 1992) focuses largely on schools, but it is of interest to us here both for the sheer number of its unsubstantiated claims, and for its sustained attack on the teaching profession. Among the claims it makes is that pupils who truant from school will live unhappy, unfulfilled lives and probably turn to a life of crime (DES, 1992, para 1.25); that regular school attendance leads individuals to be well-balanced and less likely to become criminals; that a good school ethos is dependent on deep parental involvement. These might be described as common-sense assumptions, but not as incontrovertible truths. In this paper, however, parents are presented as the experts:

> Parents know best the needs of their children – certainly better than educational theorists or administrators, better even than our <u>mostly</u> excellent teachers.
>
> (DES, 1992, para 1.6, my emphasis)

This is a great bit of rhetoric, because what it's saying is: *There are teachers out there who aren't much good. And even the excellent teachers – well, you know, even they don't know as much about the educational needs of your kids as you do.* If you want to go for the majority vote, there are many more parents around than there are teachers! Rights are a key theme in this paper, and especially parental rights. One of these is choice – a choice over what school their child will attend. We know now, of course, with hindsight, that it wasn't parents but popular and successful schools who ended up with the choice; a choice over which pupils to accept, and which to retain after Year 11, with an eye to the league tables. Another right, says the 1992 paper, is the right to information about what's going on in schools and colleges, which, it seems to be suggesting, teachers are keeping secret in some apparently sinister plot against parents. What could it be, this secret stuff that's going on? The paper never tells us. It just says that parents

> *have a right to that information. The government is determined that they shall have it, and that it shall be given in a straight-forward and simple way – characteristic of an open society – rather than in jargon-laden, inward-looking and technical language suitable only for the professional.*
>
> (DES, 1992, para 1.36)

Well, thank goodness that the government is doing something about it – whatever it is.

There are several things going on in this passage. First, there's the presentation of government in an avuncular role, securing our rights for us like a kindly uncle. Second, there's the presentation of the *professional* – presumably a teacher – as a reactionary against whom the government must take up a struggle on our behalf. Third, there is an example of what psychologists would call *projection*: attributing one's own shortcomings to another, so that here it is the teachers, not the writers of the White Paper, who are supposedly fogging the issue through a cunning use of words.

Published in 1995, *Competitiveness – Forging Ahead* may be thought to have a questionable title for White Paper on education and training, since – in the context of qualifications – 'forging' has rather unfortunate undertones. Its key words are *rigour*, *standards* and *consistency*. The way it uses these in relationship to A levels and to GNVQs points to a distinct lack of that *parity of esteem* claimed in previous White Papers. It tells of plans to enhance *the rigour and consistency of GNVQs* (DfE/ED, 1995, para 7.40), and to ensure that *the rigour and standards of GCE A levels are maintained* (para 7.41). It's easy to miss the distinction here; but what it's saying is that that while A levels have rigour, GNVQs aren't rigorous enough. It's that old status differential between the academic and the vocational, still there despite all the rhetoric. We can still see this at work today. In June 2013 it was announced by Education Secretary, Michael Gove, that GCSEs are to be overhauled in order to remove elements of continuous assessment and introduce summative assessment by final exam alone. The argument presented for this is that it will give the qualifications more rigour. It will, of course, also differentiate them even further from vocational qualifications that, by their very nature, incorporate continuous assessment. This appears, then, to be a move not towards parity, but way from it, with the equation being presented as:

End exams = rigour (high status)
Continuous assessment = lack of rigour (low status)

As might be expected in a White Paper, *Competitiveness* attributes all successes up to this point to the government, declaring that any failures of policy are entirely the responsibility of the individual. For example, it tells us:

> *the Government recognizes that further impetus is needed, particularly to encourage individuals. It therefore intends to publish a consultation document on individual responsibility for lifelong vocational learning.*
>
> (DfE/ED, 1995, para 7.18)

The choice of the word *impetus* is also interesting here. In its sense of 'forward propulsion' it is a figurative shove. Its Latin root is a martial one; it's from *impetere* – to attack. It reinforces the idea that all the developments described in this paper can be credited to a dynamic government, pushing against the weight of a nation of complacent, if not downright indolent, individuals.

Summary so far

Up to this point we've looked very closely at the way language about vocational education and training has been utilised in landmark White Papers to promote the policy and ideology of successive governments. We've seen how persuasion is used, rather than reasoned argument, and noted that such an approach would not be an appropriate one to adopt in academic writing such as assignments for initial teacher training or continuing professional development. We've also seen how, by a close analysis of these texts, we can identify contradictions and ambivalence about the purpose and status of vocational education and training. Changing attitudes over the years have been reflected in the way that key words or phrases have changed. In the next section we're going to look at how the images and metaphors in these papers also help us to identify their underlying ideas and discourses.

Critical Thinking Activity 2

This activity gives you an opportunity to apply some of what's been discussed in this chapter so far to a textual analysis of a more recent, and equally important, White Paper: Raising Skills, Improving Life Chances *(2006). Read the extract below carefully and consider the following questions:*

» *What key words can you identify?*

» *Are there any of the same key words we identified in the earlier White Papers?*

» *What do they tell you about policy change, or lack of it?*

» *What is the attitude to colleges and to teachers?*

» *To what extent is this consistent with earlier White Papers?*

» *Do you recognise any preoccupations in this extract that are re-runs of those we've seen in earlier White Papers? If so, what are they, and why do you think they are still being presented several decades on?*

» *Who or what appears to be held responsible for improving the country's economic performance? How does this compare with earlier White Papers? Is it still the usual suspects? Can you identify any flaws in the argument here?*

You'll have noticed in this chapter how the words and phrases under discussion are carefully referenced to the appropriate numbered paragraph of the document. This is important in a close textual analysis because it enables readers to locate that part of the text and read it for themselves. If you include this sort of analysis as part of any written assignment, you'll need to reference it carefully in the same way. The paragraphs of this extract are clearly numbered, so this will be a good opportunity to practice.

Extract from the first chapter of *Raising Skills, Improving Life Chances* (2006)

4. There is much to celebrate in our FE system. We have some excellent colleges and training providers. The system has demonstrated great flexibility in adapting to new challenges, is effective in reflecting and responding to the diversity of local communities, and has a strong track record in tackling inequality and reducing achievement gaps.

5. Recent improvements in the results achieved by the education and training system owe a great deal to FE...

6. Those achievements are a tribute to the dedication, hard work and skill of all those working in the FE system. They have been supported by substantial investment. Since 1997 participation in post-16 training has expanded, with total learner numbers rising from around 4 million in 1997/8 to 6 million in 2004/5...

7. Yet despite this progress, by international standards, we face major areas of weakness. The proportion of our young people staying on in education and training post-16 is scandalously low: the UK ranks 24th out of 29 developed nations. We lag well behind France and Germany in the proportion of our young adults achieving a level 3 qualification in their early twenties. The number of adults in the workforce without the skills at level 2 for productive, sustainable employment in a modern economy is much too high: in that area we rank 17th out of 30 countries. All this makes clear that as a nation we need to raise our ambitions for skills.

8. Through the 14 to 19 and skills strategies we have already put into place far reaching reforms to address these weaknesses. But we have to speed up progress. The initial report in Autumn 2005 by Lord Leitch on the skills needs of the economy in 2020 presents a daunting picture of the rate at which other nations such as China and India are improving their skills base, and the challenge we must set ourselves if we are to keep pace. Even achieving all our current targets for raising skills among young people and adults would mean that in 2020 we would be no better than mediocre in the international rankings.

9. None of us should be willing to settle for that as the limit of our aspiration. Our aim must be to be leading the world in skills development – with virtually all young people staying on to age 19 and half going on to HE; all adults having the support they need to up-skill and re-skill throughout life; all employers seeing skills as key to their success. From this can come productivity growth that will sustain us as a leading world economy.

If you would like to read the full text of this White Paper, you can find it at www.official-documents.gov.uk/document/cm67/6768/6768.pdf

Metaphors we live by

In Chapter 1 we discussed some of the metaphors that have been used in the past to describe FE. You'll remember that a metaphor is the term we use when we describe something or someone in terms of something else that gives us a vivid picture of the person or thing or process described, but should not be taken literally. If you were to say, *I'm a wreck* or *My room's a tip* or *I was hammered* (please don't take these insults to your lifestyle personally), no one will assume what you're saying to be literally true; you're just painting a vivid picture. Poets use metaphors in more complex ways; and psychologists tell us that we sometimes use metaphors without really thinking about what we're saying, and that therefore the images we use can tell us a lot about our values and beliefs of which we're not necessarily consciously aware. Lakoff and Johnson (1980) argue persuasively that our shared metaphors – the ones we all use in common without really thinking – tell us a lot about how we see the world. One example they give is the way in which we talk about 'argument' using metaphors of war, such as *he attacked every weak point* or *I won the argument* or *I'm not taking sides* or *I came out on top*. There are ways to think about argument other than in terms of war. We could construe it as a dance, for example, or an exchange of ideas. But we don't. The way we talk about it – the metaphors we use – show that we, as a culture, think of argument in military terms, even if we don't consciously realise that we do. The evidence is there in the language. By taking this approach to an analysis of key White Papers, we can theorise about the ideas or values that may underlie the policies and are unconsciously expressed through the metaphors used.

In the 1981 *New Training Initiative* paper most of the metaphors draw, appropriately enough, on the world of building and manufacturing. There are *tools of wealth creation* (para 5); young people who need to be *equipped* (para 12). Vocational education will *lay the foundation* (para 42) and the appropriate negotiating *machinery* will be used (para 52). There is also a hint of the government seeing these reforms as a military campaign in phrases such as *pressing forward* (para 52) and *lines of needed advance* (para 61). These metaphors reinforce and are entirely consistent with the tone and intent of the paper as a whole, where the emphasis is on training for industrial recovery and effective mobilisation of the workforce. The only discordant note is struck by a metaphor towards the end of the paper which speaks of:

> An increase of public expenditure on this scale as the only way of <u>plugging the gap</u> in the training provision required.
>
> (DoE, 1981, para 58, my emphasis)

Plugging the gap is an expression usually associated with preventing a flood or inundation of some kind. A plug is usually required to prevent something pouring out or through. What seems to be required in this context is an expression such as *bridging the gap* or *meeting the shortfall* or *closing the gap*. The use of the metaphor of *plugging* conjures, intentionally or not, a panic measure in the face of impending disaster. Perhaps this is inadvertently telling us something about how the government was feeling at this time.

By the White Paper of 1986, *Working Together – Education and Training* (DES, 1986) the metaphor of the building site has been well developed. Educational institutions have the task of *laying the foundations* (para 2.1) upon which post-16 learning *should build smoothly and constructively* (para 2.8). Scattered through this paper are *bridges* and *ladders* (paras 2.12, 2.15, 3.1, 5.12, 5.38), sometimes separate, sometimes together, the effect of which – and surely unintended – is to make the route to vocational qualifications sound like a dizzying business. The other main metaphor running through this paper is that of a linear race against dangerous competitors who are *pulling away from us and we must overtake them*. There must be *no going back over ground already covered*, but rather *major advances* (paras 1.7– 1.9). This race may even be a hurdle race, although there is an intention that *unnecessary barriers are removed* (para 1.9). This race against dangerous opponents, involving ladders and bridges, upon which our survival as a nation depends, can, we infer, only be won if we are *Working Together.* The word *working* is therefore metaphorical here in the sense of pulling together. A growing percentage of the population, we know with hindsight, will still not be *working* in the literal, employment sense at all.

The language in *Education and Training for the 21st Century* (DES, 1991) draws once again on industry and the building trade. Again, there are a lot of *ladders* (for example, paras 2.9, 3.1, 10.2) and some *foundations laid* (para 2.1). We *build on* (paras 3.1, 6.8, 8.8) some things, while others are *in the pipeline* (para 8.5). And again there are metaphors of conflict and combat. Colleges must *rise to the challenge* (para 9.12); there will be a search for *recruits* (para 10.2); and these will *engage in training* (para 7.1). The government will again be *removing barriers* (para 4.2) and putting business *in the lead* (para 5.3). And again, with the *Competitiveness – Forging Ahead* White Paper (DfE/ED, 1995) we are still on that building site, with *firm foundations, underpinnings* and *benchmarking* (para 7.5). The *forging* of the title conjures up the honest blacksmith (but also – and clearly unintentionally – the shabby counterfeiter).

Critical Thinking Activity 3

What impression do these metaphors give you about:

» *how the policymakers responsible for the White Papers view vocational education and training?*

» *how the policymakers see their own role in relation to colleges and learners?*

» *the level of conviction behind the phrase* parity of esteem?

What we say and how we say it

CASE STUDY

Here is a head teacher of a school talking to Year 11 pupils about possible routes of progression. Look carefully at what she says about FE, and particularly at the metaphors she uses.

Now, at the end of this year you're all going to have to make some very important choices about what you do next. Some of you will decide to stay on at school to take A levels and go on to university and achieve great things. Some of you will decide that A levels aren't for you and that you'd be happier doing something more work-related. So you'll prefer to go to the FE college and do something more practical which doesn't have so many exams and so on. And there's others of you who just haven't decided yet what you want to do, whether to aim high for university or take some other route. So what I want to talk to you about this morning are some of things you'll need to think about to help you decide which track to take. Now, if you're thinking about taking the A level track you'll need to be aiming for at least five good GCSEs. By 'good' I mean A stars, As and Bs, with A stars or As in the subjects you want to study in Year 12. OK, I can hear some of you sighing, but that's the level of achievement required if you're going to go down that track. It's no good hoping to do A levels if you achieve badly in Year 11. You'd only be miserable. You'd be much happier taking the other, alternative track – leaving school and going to college to get some practical qualifications. It's all about horses for courses. Now if you have a job in mind, that's one way to make your decision. If you're setting your sights high and aiming to be a doctor or a lawyer or a member of any other profession like that you'll need a degree. You'll need to compete for a university place, and to do that you need outstanding A levels. This school has an excellent record of A level success and university entry. Some of you, I'm sure, will go on to be our new stars in the academic world. If you're aiming to be a plumber or a hairdresser, one of those useful sorts of jobs that don't require a degree, you won't have quite such a hard climb ahead of you. If exams are your weak point you can choose a vocational course where there are no exams at all and where you can be working hands-on right from the beginning. The local FE college offers all sorts of courses like that. And if you're one of those people who hasn't enjoyed school much you'll probably find something vocational will suit you much better; not much writing and a chance to really get your hands dirty...

Oh dear. We'd better stop her there, I think.

Critical Thinking Activity 4

From your reading of the head teacher's progression advice:

» What impression do you gain about her view of the sector?

» What words, phrases or metaphors would you cite to support your view?

If you've not done so already, look online at the full text version of the 2006 White Paper, FE Reform: Raising Skills, Improving Life Chances, www.official-documents.gov.uk/document/cm67/6768/6768.pdf

» What does the title tell you about how the government's argument around raising skills has shifted ground since the 1980s and 1990s?

» Look specifically at Chapter 4: A National Strategy for Teaching and Learning in FE and identify the keywords. You may do this through a close reading, or by pasting this chapter into Wordle to produce a word cloud. What do the key (most frequently used) words tell you about whether or how FE-related policy has shifted ground since the landmark White Papers of the 1980s and 1990s?

You may also find it interesting to look at the 2013 Schools White Paper, The Importance of Teaching, www.education.gov.uk/schools/toolsandinitiatives/schoolswhitepaper and compare its key words with those found in the FE White Papers that we've been discussing. Is there a noticeable difference?

Chapter reflections

In this chapter we have closely analysed the text of some important White Papers that have marked turning points in FE over the past three decades. We have noted particularly:

» *how the recurring key words reflect the developments in FE over time as discussed in Chapter 2;*

» *how some of the key words employed change over time as policy develops; and how some remain constant, reflecting the underlying ideology;*

» *how close attention to the use of language can identify contradictions and confusions in the policy narrative;*

» *how metaphors can be seen to signal underlying values, beliefs and preoccupations that may not be directly articulated.*

We have also seen the importance of clear and detailed referencing to specific pages or paragraphs when presenting a detailed analysis of a text or part of a text.

Taking it further

The earlier White Papers listed here were originally published in hard copy, as you can see from the references, since these were pre-internet days. You can find full text versions online now in various places by entering the title into your search engine, and you may find it interesting to select one or more of them for further reading.

HMSO stands for Her Majesty's Stationery Office through which government publications such as these were issued.

If you would like to read further about how metaphors both shape and reflect the way we think about the world, I can recommend Lakoff and Johnson's (1980) book, referenced in the list below. It's quite short, and written in a very accessible style. It's certain to get you listening very carefully to things people say!

References

Ball, S.J. (1990) *Politics and Policy Making in Education*. London: Routledge.

Department of Education and Science (1986) *Working Together – Education and Training*. London: HMSO.

Department of Education and Science (1991) *Education and Training for the 21st Century*. London: HMSO.

Department of Education and Science (1992) *Choice and Diversity*. London: HMSO.

Department for Education and Employment Department (1995) *Competitiveness: Forging Ahead: Education and Training*. London: HMSO.

Department for Education and Skills (2006) *Raising Skills, Improving Life Chances*. www.official-documents.gov.uk/document/cm67/6768/6768.pdf

Department of Employment (1981) *A New Training Initiative: A Programme for Action*. London: HMSO.

Lakoff, G. and Johnson, M. (1980) *Metaphors We Live By*. Chicago and London: Chicago University Press.

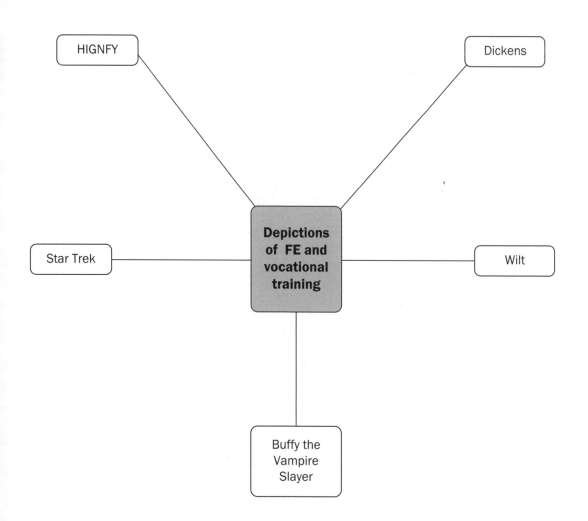

Chapter aims

This chapter is designed to help you gain an understanding of:

*   how the image of FE in fiction and other media both reflects and perpetuates the way people regard the sector;

*   ways in which such stereotyping can be recognised and challenged.

Introduction

In this chapter we're going to look at the ways the FE sector is portrayed in popular literature, television and other media. We'll be considering what these images tell us about the way vocational education and FE colleges in particular are regarded in the popular imagination. And we'll be discussing the impact that these stories may have in perpetuating widely held notions about the sector's purpose and status. One of the aspects we'll be exploring is whether, or to what extent, the portrayal of the sector has changed over time. We saw in Chapter 2 how some current ideas about the standing of vocational education have their origins in nineteenth-century beliefs about class and social structure. By examining how authors and screen writers have depicted the sector in fiction from that time up to the present day, we'll be able to see whether there has been a shift in attitude over time, or whether some of the same prejudices and value-assumptions about FE are still apparent in the way it is presented in novels and on television, even today.

You may wonder just what we can learn from looking at fictions. They are only stories, after all, aren't they? But we have philosophy on our side here. Aristotle, one of the great Greek philosophers, argued that we create fiction as an imitation of life in order that we can examine life more easily, and also so that we can see what other possibilities, what alternatives, there might be to the way things are. The eighteenth-century French philosopher Voltaire claimed that while history is an account of facts that are represented as being true; fables are an account of facts represented as fiction. What he means by this is that there are broad truths – about human nature, about society and its structures, and so on – that stories can bring vividly to life in order that we can reflect on them. And a modern philosopher, Richard Rorty, argues that one of the virtues and purposes of fiction is that it helps us to develop empathy by showing us the world through the eyes of others. In this chapter we shall be using stories in all of these ways.

Mr Squeers and 'vocational education'

We'll start with Charles Dickens. His novels present us with a picture of early to mid-Victorian England, a period when ideas about 'useful knowledge' and the relationship between education and work were being hotly debated, as we saw in Chapter 2. Dickens himself was a great admirer of the Mechanics' Institutes for the opportunities they provided for working men to improve their prospects and educate themselves out of poverty; and he threw his energy into supporting them. In 1847, for example, he travelled to Leeds to speak at the mechanics' institute there. His biographer, Claire Tomalin, tells us that his purpose was to address them:

on the subject of education, and praise their work, which included day and evening classes in chemistry, French, German, business studies, drawing and design; they had set up a good library, and attracted steadily increasing numbers of women students. An audience of several thousand...clapped and cheered many times in the course of his speech, which was a passionate endorsement of the value of educational work being done there.

(Tomalin, 2011, p 199)

But it's clear from his novels that he saw only too clearly how the notion of education for work could be abused if its only purpose was to equip learners with manual skills to serve the workforce. Take, for example, his portrayal in *Nicholas Nickleby* (first serialised 1838–39) of Mr Squeers, head teacher of Dotheboys Hall, a school for 'unwanted' boys. Nicholas has arrived at the school to take up the post of assistant teacher, and Mr Squeers is explaining to him the curriculum, while at the same time demonstrating his own teaching style. Entering the classroom, Squeers demands:

'Where's the first boy?'

'Please sir, he's cleaning the back parlour window.'

'So he is to be sure. We go upon the practical mode of teaching, Nickleby; the regular education system. C-l-e-a-n, clean, verb active, to make bright, to scour. W-i-n, win, d-e-r, der, winder, a casement. When the boy knows this out of the book, he goes and does it...Where's the second boy?'

'Please, sir, he's weeding the garden,' replied a small voice.

'To be sure,' said Squeers, by no means disconcerted. 'So he is. B-o-t, bot, t-i-n, tin, bottin, n-e-y, ney, bottiney, noun substantive, a knowledge of plants. When he has learned that bottiney means a knowledge of plants, he goes and knows 'em. That's our system, Nickleby; what do you think of it?'

'It's a very useful one, at any rate,' answered Nicholas.

This, of course, is the sort of caricature that Dickens excelled at. It is not a piece of documentary-style reportage (at least, we have to hope not), but an exaggeration for comic effect of an attitude that was prevalent at the time among the more affluent classes: that if the poor were to be educated at all, they should be educated to be useful. (Did you notice Nicholas' jibe at 'useful' knowledge?) Squeers calls this *the practical mode of teaching*. Today we might call it a *competence model*. And certainly it appears to do what it's intended to do: it equips the learner with useful skills. But what Dickens is making us think about here is: useful to whom? And the answer in this case is: to the inventor of this 'practical' curriculum; because it ensures that Mr Squeers gets his windows cleaned and his garden weeded for free. But of course, it's not just Mr Squeers who supports this idea of what vocational education should look like; it's rich and powerful employers in general who have defined 'useful knowledge' for the working classes in a way that serves their own purposes. We can understand more fully what Dickens is satirising in this scene when we understand the exploitation of learners by Mr Squeers as representing the wider power relationship between the working classes and the powerful employers who control the only curriculum on offer to them.

A further target of Dickens' satire in this passage is the ignorance of the very person who controls and delivers the curriculum. Squeers cannot spell. He, himself, is not sufficiently 'educated' even to be classed as literate. And yet he occupies this position of power in relation to the learners. The only possible outcome of this, Dickens seems to be saying, is that ignorance will be perpetuated, and that what these boys will learn will be of no value to them whatsoever.

Nevertheless, and ironically, what we see in this scene could also be described as a partially successful lesson, in terms of meeting the outcomes. The objectives seem to have been that the students would be able to:

*   spell 'window';

*   clean a window;

*   spell 'botany';

*   weed a garden.

Clearly they don't have much hope of achieving the first and third, not with Squeers as teacher; although, according to Squeers' standards as assessor, they may be considered to have succeeded. Certainly they seem to be accomplishing the practical parts of the task – the window-cleaning and the weeding. Can Squeers, then, justifiably claim to have taught them something? This is another serious question that Dickens is asking us to consider. Is it enough that something has been successfully learnt, or is there something else – something about purpose and value, personal development and cultural enrichment – that should be taken into account alongside that notion of usefulness to employers? And if the agenda, beliefs and qualities of whoever sets the standards are not transparent, what value can we set upon achievement of those standards? The learners at Dotheboys Hall are not in a position to question either the curriculum or the competence of their teacher. They are relatively disempowered, as most young learners still are, in relation to the curriculum, the teacher and the institution. But if Squeers were to tell *you* that your spelling is fine, how much faith are you going to put in that?

Critical Thinking Activity 1

The passage from Nicholas Nickleby *highlights a number of important questions about vocational education that are still debated today. You will find them summarised here. As you read through them, reflect on your own experiences, both as a learner and as a teacher, and consider how you would answer them. You might find it useful to discuss them, and your answers, with a colleague or mentor.*

»   *In the design and content of today's vocational curriculum, whose needs are prioritised: the learners' or the employers'?*

»   *Can the 'success' of a lesson be measured in ways other than learners achieving the objectives? If so, how?*

»   *To put this another way, is a lesson where all learning objectives are achieved necessarily a 'good' lesson? Make sure you 'unpack' and explain your answer.*

» *Can you think of some examples where the unequal power relationship between teacher and learner is most apparent in FE today? What obligations does this put on the teacher in terms of their professionalism and classroom practice?*

Mr Kipps and the rat in the drainpipe

We're going to move forward in time now to the early twentieth century and consider one of H.G. Wells' characters, Mr Kipps. H.G. Wells, like Dickens, was a prolific writer who had raised himself from a relatively impoverished childhood. Wells, however, never quite achieved the social acceptability of Dickens. It is said that he never entirely lost his 'common' accent, and was therefore unable to pass as a perfect gentleman. His rather colourful personal life didn't go down too well, either, in some circles. We saw in Chapter 2 how much was made of the distinction between gentleman and worker in terms of education and curriculum. Wells had personal experience of this; and in his novel, *Mr Kipps*, he tells the story of someone whose educational opportunities and occupational horizons are constrained by his lack of money and social status. Wells shows him as a teenager serving an apprenticeship as a draper in the retail trade and explaining how it feels to have no choice, no prospects, no hope of achieving his ambitions. His employer, Mr Shalford, laments the fact that Kipps learnt nothing 'useful' at school.

'Dear dear! Pity you couldn't get some c'mercial education at your school. 'Sted of all this lit'ry stuff.'

Any non-work-related curriculum is, for Mr Shalford, simply *lit'ry stuff* – of no real use. What he is interested in is profit.

Mr Shalford, being a sound, practical business man, set himself assiduously to get as much out of Kipps and to put as little into him as he could.

This means that Kipps, who in theory should be receiving a training that will challenge and interest him, finds nothing in this on the job instruction that stimulates his enthusiasm. Wells describes how Kipps *plumbed the abyss of boredom, or stood a mere carcass, with his mind far away*. This is the very picture of learner disengagement, physically present but mentally and emotionally absent. And Kipps is not the only one to feel this way. The situation feels exactly the same to his fellow trainees, as one of them explains:

'I tell you, we're in a blessed drainpipe, and we've got to crawl along until we die.'

The metaphor of being trapped, like a rat, in a drainpipe exactly captures that sense of being coerced or constrained into a route that has not been willingly chosen, which leads to nowhere you'd want to go, and holds no interest or promise of fulfilment. Mr Kipps is not in college, but is undergoing the early twentieth century equivalent – what we would now call 'on-the-job training' and what Wells calls 'apprenticeship'. There is clearly little challenge involved, and a great deal of boredom; so Kipps' dissatisfaction is perhaps not surprising. We've seen it argued, for example in the Wolf Report of 2011, that the instrumental approach and repetitive nature of a competence-based curriculum can mislead learners into thinking of learning as a sort of tick list, with nothing to excite a deeper level of understanding or an interest in learning for its own sake; nothing of relevance to personal growth and development. Just so, the young Mr Kipps feels himself trapped in a training that he didn't choose and doesn't enjoy. He wants more out of life. More challenge, perhaps; or more hope of better things.

All of us who have worked in FE have probably met learners who feel like this; and to some extent we can see their point. An instrumental vocational training is unlikely to meet wider learning needs, such as an appetite to understand more about how the world works or what makes human beings tick; or to engage with abstract ideas and debate questions about value. These are all part of a liberal curriculum, which is not directly work-related. We have grown used to thinking of these two types of curriculum – the vocational and the liberal – as being somehow in opposition, perhaps because that is how we see them in practice. The learner either stays on at school or goes to college; the 18-year-old either goes to university or into work-based training. But they need not be mutually exclusive, as educationalists such as Richard Pring (1995; 2002) point out. Pring argues for an approach that he terms *liberal vocationalism*, capable of providing a more rounded curriculum that will serve the personal development needs of the learner as well as the practical needs of the employer. This is an argument that is explored further in Chapter 7.

You may be pleased to know that Mr Kipps breaks away from his training, just as Wells did in real life, and finds a less conventional path to the future. He still has a great deal to learn, but the difference is that he will have some choices in setting the agenda. Perhaps his is just the sort of character who would have benefited from a liberal vocationalism.

Critical Thinking Activity 2

» *The extracts from* Mr Kipps *must set us questioning whether there are elements of the vocational curriculum – or even something about the very nature of that curriculum itself – which may be an underlying cause of learner disengagement. It also raises questions about choice: would some learners opt for a competence-based vocational curriculum if there were alternative routes open to them?*

» *Imagine that you have been asked to design an ideal curriculum for your learners – one that would not only prepare them to work in the appropriate vocational area, but would also engage their interest more widely with current events, for example, or interpersonal communication, or a critical appreciation of media entertainment, or all of these and more. What would such a curriculum look like? Would the liberal element be bolted on, or would you be able to embed these broader areas of interest within the vocational curriculum itself? How would you decide what to include and what to exclude? How would you arrive at a decision about what your learners might want or need? And how would you justify the choices you make?*

You might find it useful to read (or re-read) the Wolf Report (you can access the full text online), and read some of Pring's work for yourself to help inform your curriculum design. You'll find references to help you at the end of this chapter.

Wilt meets Meat One

We're going to move forward in time now to the 1970s, when a comic novel about the life of an FE teacher became a bestseller. The late Tom Sharpe's *Wilt* (1976) could be accused of presenting the FE college as a place where staff were cynical and students were not very bright. But it wouldn't be entirely fair to view the story as a lampoon of the sector as a whole. The main character, Wilt, is a teacher of liberal studies. This alone tells us that the novel is set at a time when the vocational curriculum was tempered with a broader range of learning opportunities. This meant that learners on vocational courses would have mandatory classes in subjects such as literature, communication, and discussion of social issues, taught by staff from the liberal studies department. It was a bolt-on model of what we would today call value-added curriculum content, and it was not always popular, either with the students or with their vocational teachers. Here we have a summary of Wilt's afternoon:

> At five to two he went down to Room 752 to extend the sensibilities of fifteen apprentice butchers, designated on the timetable as Meat One. As usual they were late and drunk.

There are two things in this short passage that are worth exploring more closely. First is that phrase *extend the sensibilities*. What is he talking about here? Well, one of the claims made for a liberal (as opposed to vocational) curriculum is that it does introduce opportunities for the learner to engage with, and respond to, the creative arts such as literature, film, painting and so on. Developing an ability to understand, relate to, and be moved by these areas of human creativity is what is meant here by *extending the sensibilities*. What Sharpe is doing, for comic effect, is using this phrase in conjunction with *apprentice butchers*. This is only funny if there is a shared assumption that butchery and artistic sensibility are an unlikely combination. What's being implied here, it seems, is that a curriculum that seeks to extend the sensibilities of people who aim to butcher meat for a living is ridiculous enough to make us laugh. Dissecting any joke is enough to kill it, of course. But it's important that we understand what's driving the humour here. This is a joke that takes for granted a shared view of vocational students as limited and insensitive – even brutish. This is reinforced by their name on the timetable: 'Meat One'.

And what else do we learn about these FE students? That they are habitually *late and drunk*. In other words, it's not simply that their teacher, Wilt, is presenting them in a negative light because of his own prejudices. On the contrary, their behaviour is depicted in such a way as to reinforce Wilt's view of them. Anyone who's worked in FE knows that learners can be unpunctual. But turning up drunk? Not so much (although perhaps not entirely unheard of). So what we have here is not simply comic fiction, it is satire. And what it is satirising is the attempt to deliver a strand of liberal curriculum to vocational students who do not, in Sharpe's view, want it, need it, nor – possibly – deserve it.

There's a great deal going on here. First, as you'll have recognised by now, we are encountering a view that seems diametrically opposed to that of the liberal educators such as Pring who argue the need for liberal components in the vocational curriculum. The picture Sharpe gives us of FE in the 1970s when liberal studies did form part of the curriculum is one where such provision is seen as a waste of time by students and teachers alike. But we must remember that the model operating in the 1970s was very much a bolt-on arrangement, which made it easy for learners to regard it as an irrelevant extra; whereas Pring argues for an integrated model of curriculum delivery. Second, we have the issue of stereotyping. Wilt's students are learning to be butchers. It's an interesting choice that this vocational area has been selected to stand for vocational learners as a whole. Butchery is bloody, physical work, as far removed from a desk job as it's possible be. It is work where 'sensitivity' would not be an advantage – rather the opposite. And it is also, on some level, suggestive of the sort of skills that our primitive ancestors would have needed to survive: killing animals, carrying them about, chopping them up. Wilt doesn't actually refer to his students as savages; but the implication is there, not far below the surface, that these are creatures on whom lessons in literature appreciation are not only wasted but a ridiculous idea in the first place. This buys in to all the worst aspects of stereotyping vocational education and its learners that we explored in Chapter 2, and takes them to an extreme for the sake of humour. However, there is also an argument that representations of this kind, however humorously intended, don't only draw on prejudices about the sector but also serve to perpetuate and reinforce them.

The role of the sector is brought into question, too, when Wilt imagines someone voicing the view that there should be parity between vocational and academic qualifications, and that FE colleges (then known as technical colleges or techs) helped to provide a more cohesive and inclusive society. Notice how he gives her a vocabulary which makes both her and the views she expresses sound pretentious.

> ...he would end the evening with some ghastly woman who felt strongly...that intel-
> lectual achievement was vastly overrated and that people should be oriented in a
> way that would make them community co-ordinated and that's what Techs were
> doing, weren't they? Wilt knew what Techs were doing. Paying people like him
> £3500 a year to keep Gasfitters quiet for an hour.

Yes, £3,500 was a good salary in the 1970s. And yes, Wilt obviously teaches gasfitters, too. But the point to note here is that not only is the liberal, inclusive position on education and training being mocked, but that Wilt sees his job as nothing more than babysitting – keeping learners *quiet for an hour*. *Wilt*, the novel, gives us a glimpse – a caricature – of FE three years before the first Thatcher government came to power in 1979. It gives us some insights into the prejudices and preconceptions about vocational education that were around at that time, and this in turn helps us to understand the context for the radical changes that over-took FE in the 1980s and 1990s, which included an end to liberal studies and the rise of competence-based training.

Critical Thinking Activity 3

Here are some reflective exercises that you may find useful to discuss with a colleague or mentor, or record in a reflective journal, diary or log.

The extracts from Wilt *allow us to explore the caricature and stereotyping of FE learners. A caricature is where the characteristics of an individual or a group are exaggerated – usually for comic effect. Think of political cartoons or – for those of you with long memories – the puppets on* Spitting Image. *To stereotype someone is a way of categorising them or attributing characteristics to them that make them part of a preconceived type, rather than seeing them as they really are.*

» *Can you think of an occasion when you have heard or seen someone caricaturing or stereotyping FE students? Have you ever done this yourself?*

» *In what contexts can stereotyping of FE and its learners perpetuate misconceptions and prejudices about them? For example, do you think this could be an issue sometimes in relation to progression advice in schools?*

» *Could stereotyping of FE learners become a self-fulfilling prophecy? In other words, could the idea that FE learners are less academically able influence recruitment trends? There is some interesting literature you could look at here. For example, according to the Foster Report (2005), colleges of FE recruit a much higher percentage of students from lower socio-economic backgrounds than sixth forms and sixth form colleges do. And research also suggests that those learners who enter FE from a middle-class background tend to be those who have not achieved well academically in school (Thompson, 2009).*

Buffy and her gang

Although we may take issue with Wilt over whether the impression he gives of FE is accurate, we can acknowledge that the scenes he portrays are set in some semblance of the real world. The next story we're going to consider shows how stereotypes about vocational education and the status of its learners are so embedded in our culture that we even find them cropping up in fantasy fiction. *Buffy the Vampire Slayer* began as a feature film and was subsequently made into a TV series that ran from 1997 to 2003. Created by Joss Whedon, it follows the adventures of Buffy and her gang; all American high school students who, as the series progresses, grow older – as might be expected – and begin to consider their post-school options (while conducting a campaign against vampires and a range of other hostile super-naturals on the side – obviously). On the whole they are a bright bunch and seem to succeed at school despite their nocturnal adventures. The aim for most of them is to go to 'college', the American equivalent of university and not to be confused with FE. One of the gang, how-ever, takes a different route. This is Xander Harris. When they all leave school, Xander doesn't go on to higher education like the others, but to a community college (the closest American equivalent to FE) to learn carpentry and construction. On the surface this appears to be a fair representation of diversity and a positive model for young viewers who may also wish to follow the vocational route. But when we look more closely, what do we find? Well, not only is the character of Xander Harris the only member of the group of friends who doesn't go on to study in higher education, he is also the only one from a working-class home.

This conforming to stereotype can be seen as a reflection of how things are in reality, which serves to make the world of Buffy more convincing and helps us, the viewers, to suspend our disbelief in monsters and the undead so that we can enjoy the show. But what it's also doing is perpetuating the idea that vocational education is for the less academically successful learners, and also that it is a sort of failure. Listen to what Xander says about it:

> *I've spent seven years seeing my friends get more and more powerful...And I'm the guy who fixes the windows.*
>
> (Joss Whedon, *Buffy the Vampire Slayer*, 1997–2003)

This idea of the vocational route as the second-best, or even as a failure to be avoided, is very deeply ingrained, largely for reasons that we explored in Chapter 2. It is something that we, as teachers, have to combat every day, much as Buffy and her gang have to combat the vampires. And, like the undead, it just won't seem to lie down.

Critical Thinking Activity 4

Xander's lament reminds us that in the current economic climate, where vocational qualifications often don't guarantee success in the job market, learners in FE are often all too well aware of the low value placed on the qualifications that they are working for. This point is made clearly in the Wolf Report (2011).

» *Bearing this in mind, consider what measures could be taken at each of the following stages and levels to address the cycle of low self-esteem, lack of parity and lack of confidence.*

a) *Schools' advice and guidance on progression.*

b) *The front line FE teacher.*

c) *FE senior management and boards of corporation.*

d) *Employers, locally and nationally.*

e) *The inspectorate.*

f) *National government.*

To boldly go?

From fantasy set in the present day we move to science fiction set in the far future. Do current assumptions about the relative value of the vocational and academic routes through education follow us even there? Into the twenty-third century? Well, let's eavesdrop on a conversation between Jean-Luc Picard, captain of the starship *Enterprise*, and the young ensign, Wesley Crusher, during an early episode of *Star Trek: The Next Generation*. They are flying a shuttlecraft to a star base where Picard is to undergo a medical procedure and Wesley is to sit an exam. Their conversation goes something like this:

> *Picard: Did you read that book I lent you?*
>
> *Wesley: I haven't had time.*
>
> *Picard: There's no greater challenge than the study of philosophy.*
>
> *Wesley: But it won't be in my exams.*
>
> *Picard: The important things never will be. Anyone can be trained in the mechanics of piloting a starship. But it takes more. Open your mind to the past: Art, history, philosophy – then all this may mean something.*
>
> (Star Trek: The Next Generation, series 1)

Anyone can be trained in the mechanics of piloting a starship. But it takes more...Art, history philosophy... Here Captain Picard is articulating the view of those who argue for a liberal vocationalism. To be 'trained' in a set of specified skills is not enough. To derive meaning from our existence we need to open our minds to abstract ideas, to beauty, to a sense of history. He is not saying that vocational education (in this case being trained to pilot a starship) is low status. He is saying that on its own – without developing a more general thirst for knowledge and understanding – a purely instrumental training cannot be sufficient if the individual is to make the most of their potential. This is not an either/or argument. We know, from the captain's chosen profession, that he also places a high value on those practical competencies that enable his crew to fly their craft. What he seems to be offering is a balanced view: that neither the vocational nor the academic will ever be sufficient on their own, and so what is needed is a combination of the two. Eventually – although we may have to wait another few hundred years – we appear to arrive at something approaching parity of esteem for education and training.

Picard says something else, too, which is relevant to our theme. He says that *the important things* will never be the subject of exams. This is a very sweeping claim, reminiscent of Carl Rogers' bold statement that nothing that is important can be taught (Rogers, 1983). What are we to make of this? Perhaps what Picard is saying here is that complex, deep learning can't always be measured or assessed. We work today in an assessment culture where there is much debate about the advantages and disadvantages of teaching to the test. If we make assessment central to learning, as a competence-based curriculum requires us to do, we will only teach what can be observed and reliably assessed. But some learning is not so easy to assess: the acquisition of values, an understanding of one's place in the world; the ability to empathise with co-workers, the poor, the elderly. All these are important aspects of working and living a fulfilled life. But, in an assessment-driven curriculum, if we can't assess them, they don't 'count', and there is a danger therefore that they may appear – to our learners at least – to have little value.

If you think back to Chapter 2 and remember the very clear distinction made in the nineteenth century between 'useful knowledge' (skills and knowledge that served the workplace) and 'culture' (acquired by gentlemen through an academic education), you'll recognise that distinction being made by Picard, although stripped of its associations with social class and economic power relationships, and therefore no longer carrying implications about status and worth. However, it pops up again in a *Star Trek* spin-off, *Deep Space Nine*, in an episode that focuses on a rather repulsive and disreputable race of aliens called the Ferengi. The Ferengi look a bit like goblins and their culture is based entirely around gathering material wealth and making profit. Lacking a moral code, they live instead by the 'Rules of Acquisition' – of which there are many – which provide guidance on how to come off best in any deal and accumulate as much profit as possible by any means they can. OK, so they sound like any old group of capitalists; but where it gets interesting is when we discover how their education system works. They don't have any formal schooling for their children. Instead, their offspring are put straight into work-based training. The series script writers are surely making a wry point here. We are presented with a race of acquisitive, wealth-obsessed cheats, completely lacking in moral compass, whose materialistic, selfish way of life is perpetuated by exposing their young to no form of education other than practical skills for work. This is taking the argument about the need for balance a great deal further than Captain Picard did! But it seems to be making the same point, that competence-based training alone cannot provide opportunities necessary for learning about values and beliefs, such as fairness, justice and generosity.

Critical Thinking Activity 5

Picard uses the word trained *in relation to learning to pilot a starship. There is probably some significance in this, because he's wanting to make a distinction between that sort of skill and the less easily observable, and therefore less easily assessable, engagement with philosophy, history, and art – all components of a liberal curriculum model. This raises some interesting questions for you to consider:*

» *Is there a real distinction to be made between what's happening when we learn a skill such as driving (OK, or flying a spaceship) and when we're gaining an understanding of philosophy or history or art?*

»   *If so, where does the distinction lie?*

»   *If you have concluded that there is a distinction, is there anything about the criteria you have used that would suggest a difference in value or status?*

»   *In your view, is a tightly-focused skills training sufficient in itself to prepare young people for the world of work?*

»   *What about those who will not be able to get a permanent foothold in the job market? Might a broader, liberal-vocational model be of benefit in enabling them to find fulfilment outside work?*

»   *Is it the role of the FE college to do anything other than provide learners with skills specific to their chosen vocational area, which may or may not include flying a spaceship? In considering this question, you might find it useful to look at the Foster Report (2005) which defined the role of FE (and what was then called the Lifelong Learning Sector).*

HIGNFY

Back to the present day, now; and fans of the programme will recognise the abbreviation of the long-running topical quiz, *Have I Got News For You*. The two team captains, Ian Hislop and Paul Merton, are from very different educational backgrounds. Hislop attended Eton and Oxford; Merton tells us he went to a secondary modern school and left at 15. They represent, in some ways, the two extremes of educational provision in the UK. But what they do with this is to make a running joke of it. If ever Hislop quotes a Latin phrase, for example, Merton declares that he, himself, has a CSE in woodwork. By drawing attention to the absurdity of this inequality they are also poking fun at the snobberies and prejudice that underlie questions of status in relation to educational provision. Merton's 'CSE in woodwork' (which we suspect may well be apocryphal) reminds us of Xander and his disappointment in himself at 'only' being a carpenter. But Paul Merton and Ian Hislop sit there on our screens as equals, one with his woodwork and the other with his Latin, exposing the nonsense behind the comparison by making a perpetual joke of it.

Chapter reflections

In this chapter we have used stories to explore a number of key questions about FE and the vocational curriculum.

»   *What or who is the vocational curriculum for; and who decides?* (Nicholas Nickleby)

»   *Are there features of the vocational curriculum itself that are responsible for learner disengagement?* (Mr Kipps)

»   *To what extent can the stereotyping of FE students become a self-fulfilling prophesy?* (Wilt)

»   *What effect do preconceptions about vocational education have on learners' self-esteem?* (Buffy the Vampire Slayer)

»   *What ideas lie behind the assumption that vocational education is somehow of less value than an 'academic' one? And what are the advantages of combining them?* (Star Trek: The Next Generation)

» *What might be the dangers of a purely instrumental training curriculum? (Star Trek: Deep Space Nine)*

» *How can these assumptions about value and status be exposed and challenged? (HIGNFY)*

Taking it further

If you found it useful to read about how FE is reflected in fiction, you might also enjoy the following book, which looks what we can learn about mentoring from novels, films and television:

Gravells, J. and Wallace, S. (2012) *Dial M for Mentor*. Northwich: Critical Publishing.

References

Foster, A. (2005) *Realising the Potential: A Review of the Future Role of Further Education Colleges*. Annesley, UK: DfES.

Morris, W. (1888/2008) *Useful Work Versus Useless Toil*. London: Penguin Books.

Pring, R. (1995) *Closing the Gap, in Liberal Education and Vocational Preparation*. London: Hodder and Stoughton.

Pring, R. (2002) Liberal Education and Vocational Preparation, in R. Barrow and P. White (eds) *Beyond Liberal Education: Essays in Honour of Paul H. Hirst*. London: Routledge, 49–79.

Rogers, C. (1983) *Freedom to Learn for the 80s*. Abingdon: Merrill.

Thompson, R. (2009) Social Class and Participation in the Further Education: Evidence from the Youth Cohort Study of England and Wales. *British Journal of Sociology of Education*, 30(1): 29–42.

Tomalin, C. (2011) *Charles Dickens: A Life*. London: Penguin Books.

Wolf, A. (2011) *Review of Vocational Education [The Wolf Report]*. London: Department for Education.

6 The Martian's eye view: what new teachers see

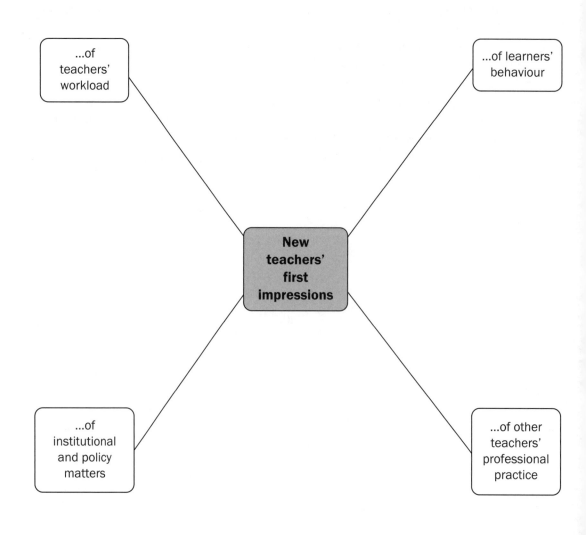

...of teachers' workload

...of learners' behaviour

New teachers' first impressions

...of institutional and policy matters

...of other teachers' professional practice

Chapter aims

This chapter is designed to help you gain an understanding of:

*   how events and attitudes within the sector appear to newcomers;

*   motivation and behaviour issues that insiders may take for granted;

*   how some of these can be addressed at the classroom level.

Introduction

Using anonymous extracts from the reflective journals of student teachers in FE, this chapter explores what teaching in FE looks like and feels like from the point of view of those who are experiencing it for the time. The journal reports will enable us to identify the main issues that student teachers find most surprising about their initial FE experience. This seeing things through fresh eyes is sometimes called 'taking the Martian's viewpoint'. It can alert us to attitudes, behaviours and events about which veteran insiders, through familiarity and custom, may grow tolerant or cynical over time.

The journals

The journal entries we'll be looking at in this chapter were all made by trainee teachers during their first weeks of experience in FE colleges. The trainee teachers – 23 women and 18 men – were aged between 23 and 47, and only four of them had previously attended FE as students. The majority were entering it for the first time and so their reports of what they see and experience give us an interesting view of the sector as seen by outsiders. They were all required to keep a reflective journal as part of the professional development leading to their teaching qualification. There's room here for only a fraction of the journal material, and not every trainee teacher is quoted. But the selection of extracts you'll find in the following sections are representative of the themes and preoccupations that dominate those journals, and they've been selected as typical and indicative. All these trainee teachers gave permission for quotes from their journals to be used this way, with a guarantee of anonymity for them, the learners and the colleges in which their experiences took place. So what we have here is a group of trainee teachers telling us, in their words, something about their first impressions of FE, its teachers, its learners, its policies and pressures. If you yourself are a trainee teacher new to the sector, you may recognise some of what they are saying. If you've been teaching in the sector for a while, you may find it useful to be reminded of what it feels like to be a 'newbie' discovering how your expectations compare with the real thing.

Critical Thinking Activity 1

Do you keep a journal of professional practice (or a diary or a log) in which to record your ideas, experiences and reflections? Making a note of happenings or conversations that feel important or significant (these are sometimes called 'critical incidents') can help us to think more clearly about what we're doing or seeing, and to use what we learn from such reflections in planning future practice.

» *If you don't already do so, try it for yourself now. Think back over your most recent classroom or workshop experience, whether as teacher, observer or student. What stands out most clearly in your mind from this session, and why? Make a note of this and then consider carefully: is there anything to be learnt from this for your future teaching? If so, what is it? These were the sort of journal entries the teachers in this chapter were making. You can see some of the things they wrote in the next section.*

Reflections about learners

It's important to bear in mind that, despite the critical tone of some of the journal entries you'll read, the predominant attitude of these trainee teachers was a very positive, enthusiastic one. They were seeing and experiencing some things that troubled them; but this didn't lessen their conviction that the sector was doing valuable work and that they wanted to be a part of it.

One of the aspects of FE teaching that clearly surprised them from the outset was the generally poor levels of student punctuality and attendance. They observed this not only in the classes they themselves were teaching, but also in the classes taught by experienced teachers that they were required to observe. In their journals they try to understand this behaviour, to work out why it might be happening and what sort of things they could try, with their own classes, to address it. One student-teacher writes:

> *After a large number of them arrived late, and several decided to go to the toilet after the start of the session, I quickly realised this was not a highly motivated group.*

Another comments:

> *The poor attendance of the first and second year students is becoming an increasing concern and the continued absence of certain students places the course's existence in jeopardy. It is difficult to know how to approach the problem as many are quite arrogant when quizzed about their attitude.*

And another, whose class was timetabled to begin at 10.30am, explains:

> *By 10.45 I had as close to a full class as I have experienced, ie five...The timekeeping of the students was familiar and underlines the problems the staff have in planning a lesson and working through the curriculum.*

What we notice about these accounts is that they don't simply report what happened, but go on to reflect on the possible implications. The first takes the very sensible line of 'reading' the students' behaviour, taking it as a communication of sorts that it is important to understand. What does it mean? And the conclusion drawn is that the lack of punctuality and engagement results from a lack of motivation. The trainee-teacher can now move on to the next question: What can be done to motivate them?

In the second extract the journal writer recognises that a possible consequence of non-attendance on this scale is that the course will be deemed to have fallen below minimum required numbers and will cease to run. Again, this is looking beyond the inconvenience or anxiety such behaviour causes the teacher, and seeing the bigger picture. In the third extract the writer makes a connection between learner punctuality and a workable lesson plan. How can teachers plan for lessons and hope to cover the curriculum content if learners habitually miss whole sections of the lesson? In all three cases we have observation, followed by professional engagement:

- This is happening.

- What can it mean?

- What can be done to address it?

Another aspect of FE that these newcomers found surprising was how commonly learners failed to complete not only tasks and activities designed to be carried out in class, but also crucial coursework that would count towards their final assessment on which their vocational qualification depended. As trainee-teachers in the early stages of their experience, they were not involved in setting or marking coursework. What they were reflecting on was the way the experienced teachers they were observing dealt with this failure to meet deadlines or hand in work at all.

For example, one writes:

> There certainly appears to be a leniency beyond any experience I have encountered and a toleration of students failing to complete assignments on time that I feel can be of little benefit to anyone.

And another comments:

> I am not sure I could tolerate the level to which some students for whatever reason fail to complete tasks.

This goes beyond surprise. There's a sense of indignation – almost of outrage – here. But why? I think the answer lies in the last line of the first of these extracts. It's because it's obviously *of little benefit to anyone* that learners fail to complete. They will leave without their qualification, and their teachers will lose the satisfaction of having supported them towards the next stage of their progression, whether that's into work or onto a further qualification. There's a sense of outrage perhaps because intentional non-completion robs the teaching–learning relationship of meaning. These trainee-teachers cannot understand why experienced teachers tolerate this state of affairs. Has familiarity made it seem less shocking? This issue of non-completion is a very good example of how a newcomer or outsider can pick up on important issues that insiders may have grown to tolerate.

This seems to apply equally to observations of learner behaviour in the classroom and workshop. One of the trainee teachers gives this vivid account of one of the first lessons he taught:

> None of the girls like to listen to anyone for more than about ten minutes. None of them like to stay for the full two hours. Furthermore all of them let you know precisely how they feel when they don't like the lesson. X starts drumming on the table and asking, 'This isn't bothering you at all, is it?' I say, 'Well, would you have liked me to drum right the way through your presentation last week?' And she says, 'Yeah.'

He goes on to reflect on what it is he might be doing 'wrong'. There is an assumption, as there is in most of the journals, that learner behaviour of this kind must be the teacher's fault – not only in the failure to address it effectively, but in somehow causing it in the first place. Perhaps when we're just beginning our teaching career it's inevitable that we would assume it was us who'd got something wrong, or omitted to do something, thereby taking on the blame for this sort of provocative or disruptive behaviour. But we know from Chapters 2 and 3 that learner disengagement can be seen as stemming from causes that are institutional, systemic or socio-economic and therefore beyond the ability of the teacher to rectify. This trainee teacher is describing classic disengaged behaviour. The learner doesn't want to listen and decides it would be more fun to try and provoke the teacher by annoying him. That way she gets his attention, but doesn't have to do any work. Perhaps he's right and she doesn't 'like' the lesson; but it's just as likely that she doesn't want to engage with it because she doesn't see the point, or is afraid it will be beyond her, or would rather amuse her friends than please the teacher. Her behaviour is certainly telling him something, but the message may not be what he at first thinks it is.

The new teachers also worried a lot about the short attention span of the learners; their unwillingness to engage with, or discuss, abstract ideas; and their lack of note-taking skills. The following brief extracts illustrate this concern:

> *It's tough getting them to listen for more than a few minutes together.*

And:

> *Their attention span is difficult to locate and their resistance to new ideas is phenomenal.*

And:

> *Blank expressions greeted their initiation to the theories, and a refusal to entertain the idea of learning such notions.*

This difficulty was encountered not only on basic level courses but also with learners working at an advanced level, as we see here:

> *I noticed that very few of them were attempting to make notes and although I'd prepared some printed handouts for them I suggested that as Advanced students they should be developing note-taking skills.*

These observations suggest that teachers new to the sector may tend to over-estimate the starting point of their students in terms of their skills for learning. The three main problems – short attention spans, intolerance of theory and lack of note-taking skills – were clearly unexpected. There was an assumption that learners would arrive in college having already acquired these skills at school. The fact that they demonstrably do not, leads one trainee teacher to question the education system. Reflecting on the learners' reluctance to think up ideas of their own when given the opportunity, she writes:

> *It was for me strange to see how difficult this freedom seemed to be for them. They were relatively happy copying the style of a given newspaper but lost when it came to creativity. Is it the result of present education policy?*

But then she adds:

> *Perhaps they just need more time.*

What she seems to be saying here is that maybe they just need more time in FE, where she can encourage them to be creative and to think for themselves. The transition from school to college doesn't automatically equip learners with a set of skills appropriate to studying at the FE level. Part of the role of the FE teacher is to help them to develop these: to gradually extend their attention span; to provide them with textual scaffolding to support the development of note-taking skills; and to recognise that working with abstract ideas and concepts may be unfamiliar, or even scary, and so it's not productive to push them into it headfirst.

Critical Thinking Activity 2

If we summarise the observations about learners that were reported in the journals, the list looks like this:

a) *Lack of punctuality and poor attendance.*

b) *Non-completion of classroom tasks and key coursework.*

c) *Disruptive or provocative behaviour.*

d) *Lack of skills for learning (sustained attention, note-taking, receptiveness to abstract ideas).*

» *Select one of these issues and decide firstly what you think might be the cause; and secondly how you would act on it if this was something you encountered in your own teaching.*

» *To what extent do you think it should be the teacher's responsibility to address or prevent these barriers to learning; and to what extent should they be seen as institutional issues to be dealt with at a college level? You might find it useful to discuss this question with a colleague or mentor.*

Reflections about teaching

We've seen what these trainee teachers noticed most about the learners they met; but what was their view of the teaching that they observed, and was there anything about that, too, that surprised them? Well, yes. The most consistent observation that emerged from their journal accounts was the extent to which the teachers they worked with seemed prepared to tolerate learner disengagement and non-compliant behaviour; and the fact that some – albeit a small minority – appeared to understand their role as simply to keep the learners occupied and reasonably quiet, without any great expectation that successful learning would take place. One trainee teacher claims that his mentor told him that the:

> *main expectation of students should be their attendance and little else – the basic role being primarily to baby-sit them through the course.*

Another gives the following account, which seems to support the first:

...during my first week I observed teachers allowing students to come and go as they pleased, talk while they [the teachers] were talking and eat packets of crisps etc. throughout the lesson.

What are we to make of this? I know from my own experience – and you probably do, too, from yours – that this is not how FE teachers typically operate. It is arguably the shock of encountering these sorts of practices and attitudes that causes the trainee teachers to give them such emphasis in their journals, rather than writing at length about the sound classroom practices they expected to, and did, observe. But this 'babysitting' approach was sufficiently present, and across a variety of colleges, for several of the trainee-teachers to comment on it. One of them, in reflecting on what she has seen, recounts asking the class teacher about it, and then begins to come up with some possible explanations:

The main issue that arose in my mind today was the students' lack of attention in two classes that I joined [as observer]. They were taught by the same tutor who tended largely to ignore the constant talking that went on throughout most of the two sessions. Low key control was occasionally attempted but not sustained. On talking to the tutor afterwards it was admitted that he feels there is little that he can do to improve the situation; if he were to try heavier methods he fears that many students would rise to the challenge and become even more disruptive. I guess there's a certain apprehension about being too heavy-handed in case it causes students to drop out, which would result in a loss of funding. Obviously this would not please management. Whilst I appreciate the tutor's dilemma, I wonder how far such bad manners from students must be tolerated. Moreover, are they actually learning anything?

There are three important questions raised here. One is about what constitutes successful strategy in dealing with disruptive behaviour. The class teacher seems to have made a conscious decision here. He is not adopting a babysitting approach, but is purposely avoiding direct confrontation that could lead to escalation. This is a perfectly valid strategy, and leads us to wonder whether something similar was happening in the problematic lessons that other trainee teachers wrote about. Perhaps they were to some extent misreading what they were seeing. Another question is about funding and retention. If teachers are under pressure to retain, for the sake of college finances, students whose behaviour constitutes a barrier to others' learning, they are left in a position where the action they can take to improve engagement is very limited. And the third question is the one posed at the end of that extract: are the learners actually learning anything? This trainee teacher is making the point here that supporting learning is what the teacher's role is all about. If circumstances prevent them from doing this, then they really are just reduced to 'babysitting'.

As well as picking up on this dramatic minority of cases, the trainee teachers were also surprised at a more mundane, although equally difficult, aspect of the teacher's role: the pressure of administrative duties, or 'paperwork', as it's still called – even when most of it involves data required electronically. What they observe is that the weight of admin seems to cause the teachers more stress and anxiety than any other aspect of their role, including managing difficult students. And a link is made between the sense of this as a burden and teachers' own self-esteem. The following extract written towards the end of the trainee teacher's first term, is typical:

It is noticeable how the staffroom is becoming more tense as the ever-mounting administration piles up and the pressure builds on staff.

This is an interesting reminder that the work of the teacher extends beyond their classroom practice; and particularly so in FE, where it is not only the admin, but also maintaining relationships with employers, awarding bodies, regulatory bodies and other relevant national organisations, which is part of their professional responsibilities. This is clearly a revelation to some newcomers, who have been imagining the role as limited to the practices of teaching, learning and assessment.

Critical Thinking Activity 3

We get a sense from these journal entries of both the perceived limits and the complexity of the FE teacher's role. It is particularly interesting to see how these trainee teachers have focused in on what is probably for them, as beginners, the most problematic and worrying aspects of teachers' work: behaviour management and the considerable administrative requirements, or 'paperwork'. In order to maintain a balanced view of the FE teacher in action, let's look at a journal entry written towards the end of a trainee-teacher's first term in college.

» *As you read it through, make a note of the qualities and skills that are identified here with a 'good teacher'.*

» *Which of these do you think can be quickly acquired by a trainee teacher?*

» *Which do you think would have to be worked on over time?*

» *What additional light does this extract throw on some of the observations quoted from journals earlier in this section? Does it enable you to arrive at any alternative interpretations or understandings?*

After two lessons team teaching with my mentor, Martin I sat back and watched him again today because I wanted to see again how he gets their attention and keeps them interested. He's very good at this. When we're team teaching I can feel the learners' interest wavering when I do my bits – and I think they probably behave themselves only because Martin's in the room. If he wasn't, I'm not sure I'd be able to keep them engaged and on task. So how does he do it? It's easy to say it's about 'presence' but what does that really mean? I've seen it with the other experienced teachers I've observed as well. It's something about a confident manner – I'm not sure how confident they feel, but they certainly look it – and about the sense that they like the learners and enjoy the subject they're teaching. So there's this sort of positive energy that comes into the room with them and it carries the learners along. It seems to make the learners like them in return and want to please them. But it's complicated, because this could make them sound all friendly and 'soft', but they're not. Look at Martin. If a learner steps out of line, Martin's got a glare he can turn on that scares even me. And he can change his voice from friendly and jokey to very cold and stern in a second if anyone's behaviour oversteps the line. I suppose there's also something about where they draw the line, these teachers. They don't pick up on every little thing, they don't go in for confrontation unless it's serious. Martin seems to know when learning is progressing ok, even if there's a bit of noise, and he doesn't interrupt that to have a biff at someone. And the thing is that when they're interested they don't tend to play up. And I've seen three ways he keeps their interest. He uses his voice in a very expressive way, like telling a story, with funny examples sometimes, like stand-up. And he always seems really interested himself, like he's sharing something that's important to him, that he's enthusiastic about. And he comes up with really good activities for them to do that they enjoy. But he always keeps the pressure on, timing them tightly, giving them a countdown to when they have to finish. This is the sort of teacher I want to be. I know it takes practice. I might have to fake the confidence at first. But I can do the enthusiasm, and I can work on all the other stuff. It feels like a real privilege to be joining a profession where there are teachers like Martin and the rest.

Reflections about policies and college structures

Because the purpose of the journals was primarily to focus on pedagogic practices, the trainee-teachers' observations about wider issues such as the impact of FE policies and the influence of institutional structures on teaching were relatively brief. But what observations they did make are interesting because they show us what institutional and policy features are most striking and evident to outsiders who are encountering the sector for the first time. For example, one of the recurring questions to be raised by these newcomers was about the impact of recruitment policy on the teacher's ability to effectively support learning. The problem they were identifying seemed to be that learners were being recruited onto courses in a vocational area that did not interest or motivate them and for which they did not in any case have the appropriate entry level skills. For example, one trainee teacher writes:

> I am forced to question what a student with obvious communication problems is doing on a course so reliant on group-based coursework.

And another makes the observation that:

> [X] is a good lecturer with experience to envy, but the class refuse to display enthusiasm or initiative, and their lack of motivation leaves him perplexed.

They are raising very important questions here about the 'fit' between learner and course of study. What they describe here may well be an unintended result of a policy of widening participation; but it can also be related back to our discussions in Chapter 3 about the issues surrounding school to college progression. We saw there the arguments suggesting that some learners do not enter FE by choice but by lack of choice. They have not actively chosen the sector nor the vocational area they will study. Work in that vocation is not, for them, a personal goal that they can feel ownership of and work willingly towards. So it takes a very skilful and dedicated sort of teacher to support these learners and give them a sense of empowerment. Someone like 'Martin', perhaps, whom we met in the previous section. What this shows us, too, is the challenge that policies such as widening participation can present to the front line teacher.

The aspect of institutional structure that was most frequently commented on was the distinction between the teaching staff and the management. This distinction was observed to take a number of forms. There was a view, for example, that the two had quite different agendas: on the one side the concerns were pedagogic; on the other financial. There were recurring variations on this theme. The teaching staff prioritized the learners' needs, while the 'management' were more interested in the needs of employers. And so on. For some this was symbolised by the contrast in facilities provided for teachers on the one hand and managers on the other, as this example explains:

> *Teachers and Management seem to exist as two armed camps, in a very Marxist sense. This is reflected in the difference in accommodation – shabby staffrooms and luxurious, carpeted boardroom – the total lack of integration.*

Obviously, this clear status divide came as a surprise to trainee teachers, perhaps because everything they had read and heard about policies and models of equality and diversity and widening participation relating to the sector had led them to expect a less polarised, more collegiate and egalitarian structure for those who worked within it.

Critical Thinking Activity 4

If, as seems the case, some learners find themselves in FE by default rather than by choice:

» *What do you think are the specific skills that this situation demands of the teacher?*

» *Is it a different set of skills from those needed when supporting the learning of motivated students?*

» *Is it about skills at all, or should we be thinking here of qualities or personal attributes?*

» *If one of the results of a policy of widening participation is a rising number of disengaged learners, what are the positive advantages of such a policy? Might they be argued to outweigh the negative?*

So what did they expect?

The things that the trainee-teachers expressed most surprise about are aspects of FE that anyone familiar with the sector will recognise as being part of the working environment – but *only* a part – and a part that for some, constitutes what is most challenging and exciting about a career as a teacher in college. Yes, there are learners who find it difficult to meet the demands of the course they are on and don't feel particularly motivated to attend or engage. And yes, the standards of behaviour can sometimes appear a barrier to learning and a challenge for the teachers who have to address them. But this is to do with the nature of the sector itself, part of whose role is to extend learning opportunities to those who, for whatever reason, have not been able to fulfil their potential at school. At its best it provides an environment and ethos which are quite different from that of compulsory schooling and which therefore offer an opportunity for some learners to make a new start, with new curriculum and alternative ways of learning.

Implicit in the journal observations is the ideal FE that the trainee teachers expected and hoped to see. This is a sector in which:

• learners would be able to respond confidently to the level of work required by their course, and would engage willingly and enthusiastically with their learning;

• learners would interact with one another and with their teachers positively and in such a way as would not create a barrier to learning;

- teachers would make it clear to learners that they expected and required appropriate behaviour, and would always model such behaviour themselves;

- the clear focus of teachers and learners would be on achieving the specified learning objectives.

These are reasonable expectations, and for those of us who are involved with FE this is what we see in colleges most of the time. For anyone entering the profession – and for those already in it, come to that – this is a useful set of descriptors to keep in mind. It reminds us of what we are aiming for, and why; and it helps get us back on track if, on a bad day, things don't appear quite as rosy as that.

Critical Thinking Activity 5

» *Taking that list of descriptors above, which are an attempt to summarise FE at its best, consider what bullet points you would like to see added to it, and why. Do you think there should be something on there about teaching methods, for example? Or engagement with employers or the work environment? You might find it useful to discuss the list with a colleague or mentor and to compare ideas on how it might be extended.*

Chapter reflections

In this chapter we have looked at what trainee teachers have to say about their initial impressions of teaching in an FE college. We have discussed the observations they make about:

» *learners' punctuality and attendance, attitudes to coursework, in-class behaviour, attention span, difficulty engaging with theory and lack of note-taking skills;*

» *some teachers' low expectations of students and high levels of tolerance for lack of engagement, and the amount of admin teachers are required to do;*

» *the impact of policies, such as widening participation, on the teacher's role; and the hierarchical structure of colleges as institutions.*

From their observations we have constructed a picture of what FE provision should look like as an ideal, and presented this in terms of targets we can aim for.

Taking it further

If you would like to learn more about keeping a reflective journal, and about reflective practice in general, you could read:

Rushton, I. and Suter, M. (2012) *Reflective Practice for Teaching in Lifelong Learning*. Maidenhead: McGraw Hill/Open University Press.

If you would like to look at more first-hand accounts of teachers' experiences in FE you will find many more explored in:

Wallace, S. (2011) *Teaching, Tutoring and Training in the Lifelong Learning Sector* (4th edition). Exeter: Learning Matters.

7 Playing up and dumbing down? From liberal studies to functional skills

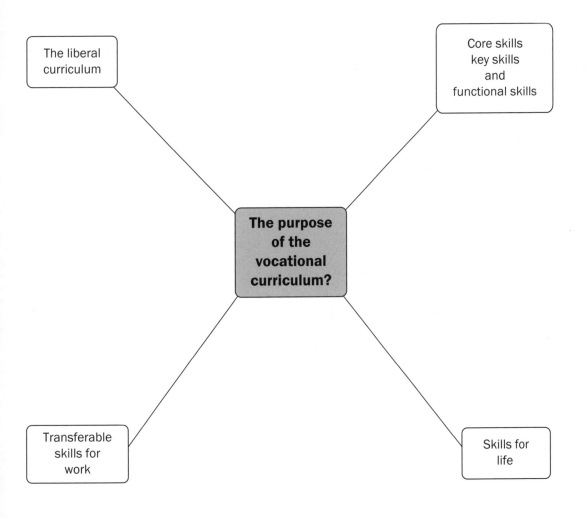

The liberal curriculum

Core skills key skills and functional skills

The purpose of the vocational curriculum?

Transferable skills for work

Skills for life

Chapter aims

This chapter:

- poses the question of what we mean by a vocational curriculum, whether it should focus only on job-specific competence and knowledge or encompass a broader range of content aimed at enriching learners' life experience;

- traces the changes in curriculum and attitudes from the 1960s and 1970s when liberal studies – usually in the form of literature, social studies or general knowledge – was considered an integral element of vocational education, to more recent trends where the vocational curriculum has been extended instead to include core, key or functional skills;

- encourages you to explore the implications and consequences of this curriculum swerve from the cultural to the functional, and what it means for the role of the teacher.

Education or training: is there a difference?

Let's start with that old, old question that we keep returning to in the context of FE: is there a difference between education and training, and if so, what is it?

Here are two members of staff at an FE college having a discussion – well, to be honest, it's a bit of an argument – about whether they should call themselves 'teachers' or 'trainers'. Look out for the main points each of them makes. We'll be returning to these later.

CASE STUDY

Bashir: Looks like the principal's sick of this terrible weather. She's gone for a cruise round the Maldives.

Gloria: Where's that, then?

Bashir: Oh come on, Gloria! I thought you were a teacher!

Gloria: Don't get cheeky with me. And anyway, I'm not a teacher. I'm a trainer. And so are you.

Bashir: Oh no I'm not. I'm a teacher and I'm proud of it. And so should you be.

Gloria: Listen, I'm proud of what I do. Nothing wrong with being a trainer. I show them how to do a task. I explain why it has to be done that way. They have a go at doing it themselves. I point out their mistakes and how to correct them. And, eventually, with practice, they get the hang of it. They acquire that skill and the understanding that goes with it. That's training.

Bashir: Training is what I do with my dog.

Gloria: That's a terrible thing to say, Bashir.

Bashir: But it's right. Reward and sanction. Praise when he gets it right; withholding praise and correcting him when he gets it wrong. It's pure behaviourism.

Gloria: Don't be daft, Bashir. What about the army? They use training.

Bashir: Yes. But look. That illustrates my point. People can be trained to kill. But we don't say 'educated to kill', do we? And that points at the difference. Training has this suggestion of uncritically following a set of procedures without trying to question or understand.

Gloria: No. There's all that underpinning knowledge and understanding, isn't there? I train trainees, right? My trainees, at the end of their training, can do the job to a nationally recognised standard. And they understand why they have to do what they do the way I taught them. I'm not getting them to just mindlessly obey my instructions, am I?

Bashir: Aren't you? Well, good. But what's the point of a learner having skills if their behaviour or frustrations or immature attitude or lack of common sense make them basically unemployable? Because look, the thing I mean about teaching being different from training is that being a teacher, for me, means you see each learner as an individual with their own interests and potential and aspirations. What I want to do is educate, and that word originally meant something like 'to lead'. I don't see our learners as just raw material to be turned into competent workers who'll serve the economy. They're people, whose understanding of the world and their place in it is still developing. Their minds are open. They're still forming their sense of right and wrong, acquiring – or not acquiring – a sound moral compass. They're struggling with relationships – with their parents, their friends and so on. And with their own identity. They're immersing themselves in their culture – music and computer games and TV. All that. And what they need from us – and I wish we could embed it formally in the curriculum – are opportunities for dialogue and understanding that isn't restricted to how you mix cement, or whatever it is you do with them, Gloria.

Gloria: Oh do get off your soapbox, Bashir. You talk such a load of rubbish.

Clearly, they're not likely to reach any kind of agreement. Each is proud of what they do, but they have quite different concepts of what their role should be. There seem to be two main arguments going on here. One is about the needs of the learner. Gloria sees these as being about employability; Bashir believes they are wider and more complex. The other is about what we understand employability to *mean*. For Gloria it seems to be about possessing the specific vocational skills to a nationally recognised standard; while Bashir is suggesting that these skills alone are not necessarily enough to create a productive and successful member of the workforce. These two arguments form the major theme of much that follows in the rest of this chapter.

So, getting back to our original question, in a more general context than the FE college, *training* is the word usually applied to the acquisition of skills for work and is associated with learning of a practical rather than theoretical kind. But there are significant exceptions to this usage. For example, we refer to 'trainee doctors' and 'trainee teachers' – both professions that involve a substantial and complex body of theoretical knowledge as well as practical skills. So perhaps we could argue that training is about preparing the learner for a specific role, job, or profession; while education has a broader purpose in developing the individual and nurturing their potential to live a useful and fulfilled life, including, but not limited to, their life at work. If we accept this to be the case, should we then expect the sector we refer to as Further *Education* to offer its learners courses and qualifications that are not restricted to the narrow focus of specific competences for specific job roles? Some, notably Pring (1999), argue strongly that this should be the case.

Critical Thinking Activity 1

But before we go on to see what Pring has to say, one of the aims of this chapter is to encourage you to think about your own definitions and whether or how you would draw a distinction between what constitutes education and what constitutes training.

» *Below you will see a list of subjects and activities. Your task is to think carefully about the ways in which these skills are learned or acquired. Do they all need the same approach, or would you categorise them separately in some way? You might find it useful to discuss and compare your lists with a colleague or mentor.*

a) *Riding a bike*

b) *Speaking French*

c) *Bathing a baby*

d) *Counselling the bereaved*

e) *Mending a washing machine*

f) *Midwifery*

g) *Window cleaning*

h) *Playing the guitar*

i) *Archaeology*

j) *Using a sewing machine*

k) *Unblocking a drain*

l) *Caring for the elderly*

m) *Hairdressing*

» *Think carefully about what criteria you are applying in making your decisions.*

» *Are you able to identify what they are? Did you apply it consistently, or were you using several criteria to make your decision?*

Pring on liberal and vocational education

You've now had some time to reflect on the notions of education and training and whether there is, or should be, a distinction between them. Here, then, is what Pring has to say. Read it carefully. To what extent does this reflect your own view? He argues

for an abandonment of those dualisms between education and training, between thinking and doing, between theory and practice, between the intrinsically

worthwhile and the useful, which bedevils our deliberations on education. Surely if
we focus on what it means to become fully a person...then there seems no reason
why the liberal should not be conceived as something vocationally useful and why
the vocationally useful should not be taught in an educational and liberating way.

(Pring, 1999, p 183)

Unity or parity? The qualifications debate

For several decades now an interesting and sometimes quite dramatic policy debate has been going on about what an ideal education and training provision for 14–19-year-olds should look like. Spours (1993) identifies three early phases of government policy, beginning in the early 1980s, a time of rising youth unemployment, when there was a drive to develop pre-vocational qualifications as part of the college curriculum. These were 'pre'-vocational in the sense that they were supposed to prepare young people, who were not yet considered ready to do so, to progress on to vocational courses by providing them with a broad extension of their education, improve their literacy and numeracy, but would be unlike school because it was framed in the context of the world of work. An early and short-lived example was known as the Certificate of Pre-Vocational Education (CPVE). Critics saw it as a cynical attempt to mask the number of unemployed school leavers and to counter criticisms about the rising number of young people who were excluded from the post-16 curriculum. The second phase identified by Spours ran from the mid-1980s to 1990 when, he suggests, the emphasis of the debate shifted from the need to address youth unemployment to the need to establish a coherent system of vocational education. We have already explored the resulting competence-based NVQ framework and its implications in Chapters 2 and 3. The third phase, and one which is crucial to this chapter, occupied the 1990s onwards and features the setting up of a dual track system of post-16 education and training in which the academic and vocational tracks were presented as having parity of esteem, a parity that Spours describes as purely *nominal* (Spours, 1993, p 77). The dual track consisted on the one hand of the general or academic route of GCSEs and A levels, and on the other of NVQs (see Chapter 3). According to government rhetoric at the time, as we've already seen, a level 3 NVQ would be the 'equivalent' to two A levels. This proved generally not to be the case, as we have seen, since they did not have the same currency for entry to employment or higher education; nor were they accorded the same status in the perception of the public. With the introduction of the General National Vocational Qualifications (GNVQs) in 1992 the dual track system became a triple track. The GNVQ was intended to bridge the gap between the general/academic route and NVQs by providing communication, numeracy and IT skills in the context of a broad occupational area, such as health and social care or the built environment. Originally intended to be taught in schools, although rapidly picked up by colleges, they were introduced to serve several purposes: as a progression route to higher education, which the NVQ had failed to provide; a progression route into employment or on to NVQs; and as a qualification that ran parallel to the academic route and had equal status. Again that phrase, *parity of esteem*, was widely used in politicians' speeches and policy documents. Again, it never quite turned out that way. One reason often cited for this was that at the same time as the use of coursework for GCSEs and A levels was being condemned by ministers as not a sufficiently rigorous form of assessment, the assessment of GNVQs was initially entirely by continuous assessment (although 'end of unit tests' were later introduced). This contradiction in the rhetoric over the concepts of esteem on the one hand and rigour on the other may well have contributed the GNVQ's eventual demise. There is an argument that the GNVQ did actual damage to the post-16 curriculum in that it not only restricted the role of the NVQ, keeping it tightly competence-focused and undermining the original intention that it should provide a vocational progression route into higher education: but also because it put an end to the development of the CPVE whose curriculum had been designed to encompass a genuinely liberal model of vocationally related education.

Meanwhile, efforts to reform the academic track of the post-16 curriculum at the end of the 1980s foundered in the face of government opposition. Despite the two main recommendations of the Higginson Report (1988) – that A levels should be replaced by a broader and balanced programme of five subjects and that there should be national guidelines on how subjects were to be combined – no changes were made. There was – and arguably still is – enormous resistance to any change in the A level system, often referred to as 'the gold standard' of post-16 education. Calls for the reform of the vocational track aroused much less controversy, which may help to explain the upheavals in the FE curriculum at that period. Nevertheless, in the view of many critics at the time, the whole of post-16 provision was well overdue for reform, and this served to fuel the policy debate. Some of those who spoke up for the reform of the 16–19 curriculum in the last two decades of the twentieth century cited the French and German models as examples of good practice. The baccalaureate, which is the national qualification for school leavers in France, allows students to follow a broad curriculum, combining subjects from the arts, humanities and sciences. Or they might choose the *baccalaureate technologique* or the *baccalaureate professionel*, which prepare students for direct entry into employment. Although it is not really the case, as some argue, that these three are considered completely equal in status, nevertheless the qualifications carry the same generic title, and the *bacs tecnologique* and *professionel* include aspects of a broader, general curriculum as well as the specific vocational content. In Germany the equivalent qualification is the *Abitur*, which combines both the breadth of curriculum to prepare students for employment and the academic rigour considered necessary to qualify them for university entrance.

However, in the White Paper, *Education and Training for the 21st Century* (DES, 1991), the government declared that its policy on 16–19 education and training was going to be one of establishing higher status for the vocational route. Critics, who would have liked to see a move towards an integrated curriculum that combined elements of the academic and the vocational rather than drawing a distinction between them, saw this White Paper as simply reinforcing this distinction and peddling the idea that a dual system was somehow inevitable. In other words, they considered this to be a missed opportunity for reform and, despite the rhetoric about 'parity', ultimately a reinforcement of the two-tier system.

And so it continues. This is basically the system we still have today. The two routes, the academic and the vocational, remain pretty much distinct. There is very little overlap. The academic route has expanded to include a few subjects that are broadly vocational, largely to meet the needs of the growing number of pupils who, because of unemployment, are now staying on at school post-16. The vocational route has, if anything, appeared to narrow and now contains very little that could be classed as general education. One route is still largely the business of schools; the other is largely the role of colleges. Nevertheless there have been, and continue to be, some small pockets of general or non-vocational education pre-sent in the FE curriculum, and that's what we're going to look at in the next section.

Critical Thinking Activity 2

In 2012 the Secretary of State for Education, Michael Gove, proposed replacing AS and A levels with a British version of the baccalaureate, which would provide a broader, more eclectic range and combination of subjects for post-16 students. He was forced to back down by a general outcry against this plan. It may be that you remember the controversy well; and certainly this is recent enough, in terms of history, for news reports of the event and the debates surrounding it to be easily researchable on the internet. Using this resource, find the answers to the following questions:

» *What were the arguments put forward by those who opposed the plan?*

» *Could they have been the same arguments that were presented 30 years previously?*

» *And what about the rationale offered by Gove in support of his proposal? Was there anything there about the wish to close the gap between the academic and vocational routes?*

» *And finally, was there any recurrence of those two terms that fuelled the same debate back in the 1980s and 1990s:* parity of esteem *between vocational and general qualifications, and A levels as a* gold standard*?*

Liberal studies: who wanted them and what were they for?

We saw in Chapter 2 how elements of a general or liberal curriculum were provided as part of vocational courses in FE in the mid-twentieth century; and in Chapter 5 we looked at the way this liberal studies provision was lampooned in fiction. But what did this attempt to broaden the vocational curriculum actually look like in practice to those who were involved, and how does it tie in with the post-16 debate? To get some idea of this, let's hear an account from a liberal studies teacher who's looking back on that time, and then from someone who was an FE student in the 1970s and is recalling that aspect of the curriculum from a learner's point of view. As you're reading what they have to say, you'll find it useful to keep in mind the following questions:

• On what points do the teacher and the learner agree and on what points do they disagree?

• What does each of them believe was the aim of the liberal studies curriculum?

• What impression do you get of the general level of support for the liberal curriculum across the college as a whole?

• Apart from the provision of liberal studies, what other evidence is there in these accounts that they are describing college practices from several decades ago?

INTERVIEW 1

Interviewer: So you taught liberal studies in FE in the 1970s? Tell me a bit about what that was like.

Teacher: Well, we had our own department. Lib studs it was known as for short. And it serviced all the other departments in the college – one of only two that did that. The other was the Department of Staff Development that ran the 730 [a teaching qualification for FE awarded by the City and Guilds London Institute]. So we knew what was going on right across the college. I mean, there were some departments we had good working relationships with and some we didn't. Some HoDs [Heads of Department] considered us a waste of time, and told us so, and made their views known to the students as well, so that made things quite difficult for us sometimes. You know, as we walked in they'd say things to the students like, Right lads, its lib studs next, so you can go to sleep for an hour. Things like that. Mech eng [mechanical engineering] was the worst. The staff there really gave us a hard time. And as a result of that, of course, so did the lads – or tried to. But we believed in what we doing, you know.

Interviewer: Which was what?

Teacher: Well, broadening the curriculum. Widening their horizons. Whatever you want to call it. The skills teaching made sure they could do a job. But our input was there to give them the social skills that would make sure they got that job and kept that job and were able to communicate appropriately with their line managers as well as their mates. And it equipped them to use their leisure time productively and have interests and inner resources to fall back on if they were ever out of work. And it helped them to question and understand the economic and political reasons behind unemployment so that they wouldn't just think it was their own fault and they were no good if it happened to them. All that and more, you know? We really believed we could make a difference.

Interviewer: So what form did this input take? What did the lessons look like?

Teacher: OK, well, let me tell you a typical day. What you have to remember, though, is that in those days a lot of students were also in employment and attending college to get their qualifications on what we called 'day release' paid for by their employers. And others only attended college in the evening because of their jobs. Most people had jobs in those days. So we'd all – the lib studs teachers – teach several late sessions a week. This was also because some HoDs liked to timetable lib studs for the last session of the day when the students would be fed up and ready for home. That was their idea of a joke. OK, so I might start the day with a class of nursery nurses where we'd be reading and discussing a novel we'd chosen together. Golding's Lord of the Flies we did, I remember; and Orwell's Animal Farm. Stories that gave us something contentious or socially relevant to discuss. And we'd link the discussion to their work, you know. And then for the second half of the morning I might be timetabled with a class of welders and we'd look at something like a warranty for a motorbike and discuss various scenarios – and whether this or that would be covered. It was a sort of comprehension exercise, really, but contextualised into something that really interested them. And we might go on to talk about customers' rights and even maybe do a bit of role play where they act the part of someone making a complaint without becoming *aggressive. That sort of thing. And then in the afternoon I might take a communication class with the business studies students, developing their communication skills by doing things like timed games where they have to share information effectively as a group so they can solve a mystery or a murder. And then maybe it would be over to the hospitality and catering department to organise their students in a debate on something socially relevant like whether the police should be armed or whether the voting age should be lower. All things to get them thinking and reading and organising their ideas in an informed way rather than just trotting out the views they've read in the paper or heard their dad spouting when he's had a couple of beers. And then the last session, the late session, that would usually be with the mech eng lads. I often used to take them out of college to visit places like the fire station, the ambulance station or the police station, where they could look at the vehicles – because that was what really engaged their interest – and have a talk from someone on duty there about road safety. Always about road safety. I like to think those sessions probably saved a few lives. We just walked along to these places. They were all in walking distance. Of course, you wouldn't be able to do that now, I don't suppose. Health and safety objections and lots of form filling. Ironic really.*

INTERVIEW 2

Interviewer: You were at FE college in the 1970s on a construction course, yes?

Student: Correct. On day release.

Interviewer: And part of your timetable for that day was liberal studies?

Student: Right. And it just seemed to us like a waste of time. They were perfectly nice and that. Nice people, You could get on with them and have a laugh and that. But us lads were there to learn a trade, not sit in a classroom like at school and discuss the lyrics of pop songs. I mean, come on. We were all working for a living. We'd left school behind. We had this one day a week at college and we wanted to get on with what we were there for, know what I mean? And our other teachers felt the same. They thought it was a waste of time an' all. And they told us so. So we obviously weren't going to take it seriously, were we?

Interviewer: Looking back, do you still think it was a waste of time?

Student: Looking back, mate, I regret a lot of things. I reckon we were lucky to have the opportunity to broaden our minds a bit, to think about the world and that, and how we fitted in. So yeah, I am a bit sorry now that we just took it all for granted and didn't make the most of it. Gone now, hasn't it? They don't get the chances we had any more.

Critical Thinking Activity 3

» *Having read these two accounts and considered them, how would you summarise the arguments for and against the inclusion of liberal studies?*

» *Their references to gender is one of the aspects of these accounts that reflect the era they are describing. Whole classes of students are referred to as 'lads', which tells us something about the way vocational areas were differentiated by gender. Reflecting on your own experience of college, consider to what extent this remains the case today.*

» *Another aspect that dates them is the title of courses referred to. Some have undergone name changes; some no longer exist. Which are these, and how do you account for this change?*

Finally, before we go on to look at the role of key, core and functional skills in the vocational curriculum, let's look at what Pring has to say about the value of liberal education and its potential for contributing to the common good:

There is a further argument which connects the liberal education of the individual with the common good. However selfish and self-centred the educated person might be, such education, liberally conceived, is inseparable from the free flow of ideas and the spirit of criticism which is the most effective bulwark against oppression and injustice...There is, then, a connection between social well-being and the pursuit of personal good through liberal education.

(Pring, 1999, p 123)

» *What do you think he means by* the free flow of ideas and the spirit of criticism ... is the most effective bulwark against oppression and injustice?

» *He seems to be suggesting that* the free flow of ideas and the spirit of criticism *are missing from a purely vocational curriculum. Do you agree?*

» *In Chapter 4 we examined the White Papers in a* spirit of criticism – *that is, critically and analytically. Can you see how this process of interrogating policy could be* the most effective bulwark against oppression and injustice?

From core skills to key skills to functional skills

We can identify two main reasons why liberal studies ceased to be a part of the FE curriculum, and both are linked to the post-16 debate. First, there was the rise of Youth Training Schemes (YTS) in the early 1980s whose curriculum of work experience and vocational skills included the transferable 'core skills' of literacy and numeracy and a subject known as 'social and life skills' in which any discussion of social, economic or political issues was proscribed. Second, there was the introduction of the competence-based NVQ curriculum that made no allowance for a broader, more general approach. However, as liberal studies declined, those core skills introduced as part of the YTS package became one of the few elements of a broader education to flourish, and soon became seen as an opportunity for creating parallels with the academic or A level route.

We can trace the origins of core skills back to a document entitled *A Basis for Choice*, produced in 1979 by the Further Education Unit, in which a core entitlement of communication, numeracy and the rather vague-sounding personal skills were advocated for all post-16 learners in FE on the grounds that these were the 'core skills' demanded by employers. By the early 1990s the promotion of core skills across the 16–19 curriculum was being presented as one way of creating a more coherent and less divisive system. It offered a way of broadening both the vocational and the academic curriculum while at the same time leaving traditional A levels largely untouched. This idea was reflected in Dearing's *Review of Qualifications for 16–19-year-olds* (1996), which, in advising how to create greater parity of esteem between the two routes, also recommended a common four level framework and a 'National Advanced Certificate', which would be awarded for two A levels or an advanced level GNVQ or a level 3 NVQ, thus emphasising equivalence rather than difference. This last recommendation was not implemented. But the core skills project did progress. Evidence suggested that their introduction into training schemes was seen by employers as a move towards meeting their needs; but there was difficulty in reaching agreement on how they could be integrated into A levels and NVQs. The GNVQ, on the other hand, appears to have been designed largely as a vehicle for delivering the core skills of communication, application of number and IT.

This was a considerable narrowing of the original concept of what should constitute core skills. For example, as early as 1974 James Callaghan in his famous Ruskin Speech included *respect for others, respect for the individual* among the desirable core skills for the post-16 curriculum. However, this was excluded and has remained excluded from all succeeding lists. The National Curriculum Council (NCC) in 1990 listed six core skills areas – communication, numeracy, problem-solving, personal skills, IT and a modern foreign language. These corresponded with the core skills identified by the Technical and Vocational Education Initiative (TVEI) at around the same time. That landmark White Paper, *Education and Training for the 21st Century* (1991), which keeps cropping up in this debate, narrowed the focus to three core skills: English, mathematics and a modern foreign language. With the exception of a foreign language, all the NCC/TVEI core skills were incorporated into GNVQs, but only communication, numeracy and IT were formally assessed. The Dearing Review of 1996 referred to these as *key skills*. That term then came into common usage, replacing the term *core skills*. A Key Skills Award was eventually introduced that was offered across both the vocational and academic curriculum. As a requirement for A level students, however, it was unpopular, apparently unworkable, and therefore short-lived. In 2005 a further White Paper, *14–19 Education and Skills*, announced the introduction of the Functional Skills Award, a qualification in English, mathematics and IT for learners aged 14+ aimed at enhancing their prospects of employment or access to further or higher education. Thus, over the past few decades, vocational learners' entitlement to a broader curriculum has passed through a number of stages, growing progressively narrower and more instrumental, from liberal studies to core skills to key skills to functional skills, moving from a liberal to a functional model not only in content and purpose, but also in name. Attempts to bring the general/academic curriculum and the vocational curriculum closer together in content and status have not yet, on the whole, succeeded. The GNVQ, once seen as a bridge, has gone, along with the common application of the key skills award. FE remains focused on the instrumental and the functional. In the view of many, this is how it should be. According to others, it is overly narrow and fails to meet our learners' needs. Thus, the debate continues.

Critical Thinking Activity 4

»   *We began this chapter by discussing what is an appropriate name for someone who supports learning in FE. Should we call them a teacher, a trainer, an instructor, an assessor? Now, drawing on what you have read in this chapter as a whole, consider how the changes in the vocational curriculum over time might have changed the way we, and others, see this role. For example, as FE has moved further towards a competence-based curriculum, have the professionals within the sector taken on a role that is more heavily weighted towards assessment than teaching? Does an employer-led curriculum cast them in the role of instructors rather than teachers? Where do you see the role of the FE professional fitting into the ongoing debate about post-16 education and training?*

Chapter reflections

In this chapter we have looked at four strands of the debate about the post-16 curriculum:

» *the issue about lack of parity between the vocational and the academic routes through the system;*

» *the attempts to create some common ground;*

» *the arguments for broadening the vocational curriculum by integrating some elements of a liberal or general education;*

» *the purpose of core or key skills and how they have narrowed over time to become functional skills.*

Taking it further

If you would like to explore in more detail the argument against excluding elements of liberal education from the vocational curriculum, you may enjoy reading the book by Richard Pring listed in the references below, particularly Chapters 6 and 8.

References

Dearing, R. (1996) *Review of Qualifications for 16–19-year-olds*. London: SCAA.

DES (1991) *Education and Training for the 21st Century*. London: HMSO.

DfES (2005) *14–19 Education and Skills*. www.education.gov.uk/publications/

Pring, R. (1999) *Closing the Gap: Liberal Education and Vocational Preparation*. London: Hodder and Stoughton.

Spours, K. (1993) The Recent Background to Qualification Reform in England and Wales, in W. Richardson *et al* (eds) *The Reform of Post-16 Education and Training in England and Wales*. Harlow: Longman.

8 'The culture of respect': motivation and behaviour in FE

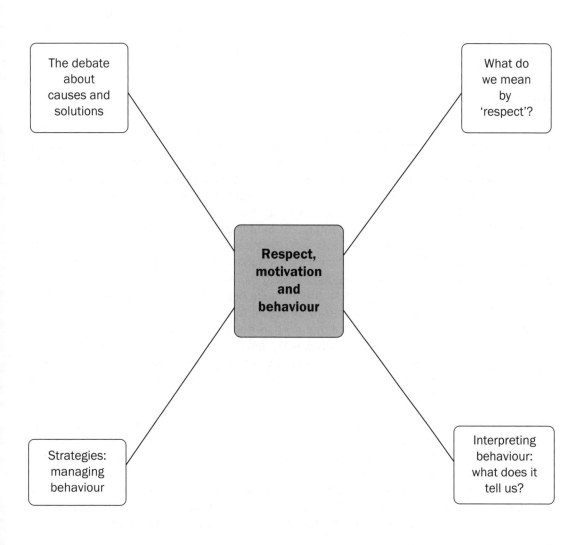

The debate about causes and solutions

What do we mean by 'respect'?

Respect, motivation and behaviour

Strategies: managing behaviour

Interpreting behaviour: what does it tell us?

Chapter aims

This chapter is designed to help you gain an understanding of:

*   the ongoing debate about learner motivation and behaviour in FE;

*   behaviours that can present barriers to learning;

*   strategies teachers use to address disengagement and lack of motivation;

*   some of the underlying reasons for learner disengagement.

Introduction

Taking as a starting point politicians' increasingly voiced concerns about the need to incul-cate *a culture of respect* in education and society as whole, this chapter examines the range of arguments and explanations that inform the current debate about those issues of motiv-ation and behaviour evident in some groups of young learners in FE. Although it questions the extent to which these should be considered exclusively as issues about learning and teaching, it also considers some practical strategies for encouraging engagement as well as exploring the traditional role of the college or training organisation in setting and policing ground rules which facilitate effective learning and teaching.

Respect

As we saw in Chapter 7, James Callaghan spoke about *respect* in his famous speech at Ruskin College in 1974, which is often seen as the starting point for the great debate about post-16 education and training. The speech hit the headlines because here was a key polit-ician talking about the necessity for education to be tailored to meet the needs of employers. We take this line of argument for granted now, but back in the early 1970s, when education was formulated largely on a liberal model and construed predominantly as a social good, a means of developing individual potential and enabling social mobility, Callaghan's spell-ing out of employers' needs was seen as signalling a significant change of direction. What he was understood to be saying was that schools and colleges were on the whole failing to equip young people with the skills needed to make them useful members of the work force. And among the 'core' attributes that he argued were necessary was an attitude of respect. Again, the implication was that teachers were failing to inculcate this in their learners; that discipline in the classroom was lax and that schools and colleges were turning out an unruly generation of youngsters. Remember, this was the era of punk. Perhaps that had some bear-ing on the public's response to what Callaghan was saying. But certainly that one speech, delivered to a relatively small audience in one college of Oxford University, sparked a series of arguments that continue to this day.

But what do we mean by 'respect'? It's a reasonable guess that Callaghan was talking about compliance in the classroom, which could later be translated into compliance in the work-place. 'Compliance' means doing what you're told. It's very close in meaning to 'obedience', although you can comply unwillingly without necessarily agreeing with what it is you're being asked to do. Of course, some would argue that education should be about teaching people to question and to think for themselves rather than just to do as they're told; and we'll come back to this point later in the chapter. But 'respect' implies more than just discipline or following orders. We talk, for example, about respect for property or for the law; respecting the rules of the game and respecting other people's rights. So it's a term, really, that encapsulates a certain attitude towards others, towards our social interactions and the way we conduct ourselves in the various aspects of our lives. It's not simply about saying a polite 'Good morning' to Mrs Featherstone down the road. We can speak to her as politely as we like, but if we then go and kick her dog, steal her bike and spray insults all over her front door, we can hardly say we're treating her with respect. Another, more recent nuance of the word can carry overtones of threat, as in, *You give him respect, or else.* But here, too, *respect* is about acknowledging the right to existence of someone other than yourself.

One question we have to ask ourselves as teachers is whether respect is about behaviour or about attitude, or about both. Is it something we can see and assess – a sort of competence? Or is it less tangible than that – something that would fall into the affective domain, rather than the cognitive or psychomotor? Was Callaghan right to think of it as a core skill that can be taught? And – perhaps most important of all – is it the responsibility of the teacher to make sure it is learnt; or is this something that parents, and indeed society as a whole, should also take responsibility for? These are important questions and, whatever the answers, they are outside the scope of this book. You will certainly have your own view. But if we focus in on the relevance here to FE and to FE teachers, there are two important points we need to keep in mind. One is that if lack of respect – disruptive or confrontational behaviour – becomes a barrier to learning for other learners in the group, it becomes the teacher's responsibility to address it, since the prime directive of the teacher is to support learning. It follows from this that the management of behaviour, the encouragement of respect, in order to prevent such situations from arising in the first place, is in the interests of the teacher and can reasonably be expected to be part of their remit. This isn't at all the same thing as saying that it's teachers' fault that young people 'lack respect'. The second issue is that, as we have seen in Chapters 2 and 3, motivation and behaviour are considered to be a particular issue in FE, for the variety of reasons that we have already discussed. The question of respect – or positive interpersonal behaviour – and how to encourage it in learners, so that they and their peers can engage and succeed with their learning, is therefore also an important part of the FE teacher's role. Learners' lack of respect may not be our fault, as we've seen from previous chapters, but it is our responsibility to address it where we can. How we can go about doing this is the subject of the rest of this chapter.

Critical Thinking Activity 1

»   Since Callaghan's speech back in the 1970s, politicians have continued to pick up on the idea of respect, not just in the context of education but also in society in general. You might find it interesting to conduct an internet search to see how 'respect' has been used as part of the political discourse over succeeding decades. Has there, for example, been a divide on party political lines, or does it appear in the rhetoric of all parties? And who is held to blame for lack of respect? Is it always the teachers, or has the argument – outside the media at least – become more complex than that?

»   Is there a policy relating to respect in your own college? Is it something mentioned as part of a policy on behaviour? How is it defined? Who is held responsible for applying the policy? What sanctions are in place? And – if you have been at your college long enough to discover this – do they work?

Disengagement, non-compliance and challenging behaviour

Let's start off by defining our terms. When we talk about students' 'disengagement' we're referring to their failure or refusal to get involved with their own learning. This is not about being a passive learner – allowing the teacher to do all the work while the learner sits like a baby bird on the nest with open beak, taking it in. It's much less positive even than that. Disengaged students have detached themselves completely from the whole idea of formal learning. For whatever reason (and we've discussed some possible ones in earlier chapters), they simply aren't interested. This lack of motivation can manifest itself in obvious ways, such as frequent absence from lessons; lack of punctuality; failure to complete and hand in work; refusal to contribute usefully to discussions or other activities; and failure to listen to what the teacher or others are saying. All of these we can refer to as 'non-compliance'. In other words, they're not doing what they've been asked to do. Obviously this means they're unlikely to succeed in achieving the course outcomes, and it may also indirectly affect the motivation and achievement of others on the course. But non-compliance, if not handled carefully, can very easily escalate into challenging behaviour as, for example, in a case where a student is directed by the teacher to do something – to sit down, or to put their phone away, or to turn their chair to face the front – and refuses point blank to do so. This is a challenge in two senses: not only is it challenging the teacher's authority; but it is also presenting the teacher with a very challenging problem! And one of the crucial components of that problem is the knock-on effect such confrontations have on the motivation and engagement of other learners in the group.

It's useful to remember, therefore, that disengagement, non-compliance and challenging behaviour are not synonymous. Rather, they represent a sequence of escalating cause and effect. It follows, then, that if the teacher is able to engage the learner's interest and attention early on, subsequent problems may be avoided. But this is very much easier said than done, particularly as the disengagement may result from wider systemic and socio-economic factors as discussed in Chapter 3.

Critical Thinking Activity 2

»   *We're going to look now at a teacher's account of working with a group of 17-year-olds in FE. As you read it through, see whether you can identify and distinguish between examples of learner disengagement, non-compliance and challenging behaviour. Notice also how the teacher, according to his own account, dealt with each of these, and the extent to which his interventions succeeded or failed. Following it, in the next section, you'll find a detailed analysis with which you can compare your own observations. We'll call the teacher Dan.*

A CLASSROOM CASE STUDY

I took Dawn's class today because she was ill. I'd never met them before, but I got the impression from her that they were hard work. It was short notice and I didn't have a lot of time to prepare stuff. But you can't just walk into a class and wing it – that's not fair on anybody. So I took along Dawn's lesson plan, but I brought my own resources that I'd used earlier with the first years. To be honest, I thought the lesson plan looked a bit of a no-goer. Mostly teacher input or group work, both with far too much time allowed. A recipe for bore-dom, really. Sorry Dawn. So I had to do a lot of thinking on my feet to re-plan as we went along. There were 15 of them – seven lads and eight young women – sitting at three tables, one all male, one all female and one mixed. I started off by asking some questions to see where they were up to. Straight away I could see that the learners at the mixed table were answering all the questions. Three girls sitting at one of the other tables weren't even facing the front. They were all sitting more or less with their backs to me and to most of the rest of the class. All the time I was asking questions they were having a quiet conversation between themselves about some relationship problem one of them was having. They weren't caus-ing any trouble, but they might as well have not been there. The all-lads table kept offering stupid answers to my questions and then roaring with laughter as though they'd been witty or something. This was annoying and quite disruptive because sometimes they were drown-ing out correct answers from the mixed table. So in the end I said to the noisiest one, OK. Let's have a system. If you've got an answer, don't shout out; just put your hand up. *Well, he just went off on one. Effing this and effing that. The gist of it was that he had no intention of putting his hand up, and what did I think this was? School? It was my own fault. I should have thought through more carefully how to handle it. Anyway, I swerved into a quick change of activity that didn't involve hands at all. But the incident had repercussions because the mixed table, who'd been quite interested in answering questions up until then, now seemed to be watching out for the next bust-up, looking at him and looking at me and not really get-ting on with the task I'd given them, which was to look at a case study and come up with an answer to two questions. I didn't know ahead of time what their tolerance for reading would be like, so the case study was set out in comic strip form – and graphic novels are now a respectable literary genre, I'm told, so no accusations about dumbing down, please. The all-girl table made no effort to look at it. Evidently couldn't be bothered even to pretend. Didn't even pick it up, but just carried on their low key conversation. The lads' table did a lot of sneering at the comic strip, drew in a few speech bubbles of their own that I decided not to investigate, and showed no sign of discussing the questions. The mixed table did a bit of half-hearted discussion, but kept getting distracted by the laughter at the lads' table, and by keeping an eye out for another drama. Obviously it just wasn't working. I couldn't just let it go on, with nothing constructive being learnt, nothing useful being gained by anyone. So I wound that activity up and told them it might be useful and interesting if we had a discussion about rules and relationships – which happened to be the focus of one of the case study questions. Let's find out what everybody thinks, I said. And I'll start, OK? Some groans, but this was obviously something of a novelty to them, so that helped get the attention of most of them. Whoever seems to be listening best gets the next go. That's always a risk, because it raises arguments over your decision. But I have a contingency plan for that.*

The all-girl table wasn't paying much attention to any of this; they were just glancing over their shoulders now and then to see what was going on, before resuming their conversation. I said, OK. How about this for a rule: everybody sits so they can look this way and we can make eye contact when we're talking? Does that sound like a good idea? *The other two tables obviously thought it did, probably because it promised some more drama when the girls were urged to turn around. The thing was, though, that once this was agreed, the pressure came from the other learners. So, with a lot of huffing and sighing, the girls squeaked their chairs around a bit so that they could see me. And then, of course, the big argument over who went next. According to them, they'd all listened.* OK, then, I said. So we need another rule. Give me some suggestions. *And they did. We managed to have an interesting and frequently heated discussion about rules, safety at work, relationships in the workplace, personal responsibility and even the principles of democracy. And I was able to relate most of it to the case study and to the learning objectives of Dawn's original lesson. It helped that it was one of the few rooms with an interactive whiteboard, so they could all have a summary of the discussion to take away. It was one of those sessions when you know you're in the right job, know what I mean?*

Analysing what happened

In your analysis of this account, you'll have noted that the teacher encountered all three types of behaviour.

Disengagement

The girls at the all-girl table have disengaged from the lesson. They are physically present, but that is all. They are engaged in something else – their own conversation. This doesn't overtly disrupt the learning of others in the classroom. They're talking quietly. They aren't making a noise or being unruly. There might even be a temptation for the teacher to simply let them be and to concentrate on the learners who are prepared to pay attention. But this might be a mistake. Did you notice how readily the rest of the class agreed to the teacher's suggestion that he should be able to see everyone's faces? Any individual or group opting out as this group was doing inevitably affects the mood of the classroom. Learners might justifiably be asking themselves: *If they're allowed to just talk and get away with it, why should we have to pay attention?* In this way, disengagement of the few can have a negative effect on the motivation of the rest. You might have expected that teacher to start with a rule designed to address the confrontational behaviour of the learner who objected to raising his hand. But this is an experienced teacher and he understands it would be seen as unreasonable to challenge one learner in particular while a whole group are being allowed to simply opt out.

Non-compliance

The group of disengaged girls become non-compliant when they are given a task but refuse to do it. Their refusal is not confrontational. They don't say, *We're not doing that!* But they are nevertheless failing to comply with the teacher's request because they simply ignore it. Again, seeing this go unchallenged by the teacher can have an effect on the morale and motivation of the others. It's the same old questions: *If they don't have to do it, why should I?* And, *If they don't get into trouble for ignoring the teacher, why should I bother to take any notice of him?* The boys at the all-male table are also non-compliant. They, too, are not carrying out the case study task – and they're being a lot noisier about it. This also is going to affect the motivation (and, indeed, concentration) of those learners who want to work, if they're not seeing the teacher managing the situation effectively. And even the mixed table, the more enthusiastic learners, begin to show signs of non-compliance, ignoring the set task in order to watch out for another confrontation between Mr Hands-up and the teacher. So we see here how lack of motivation can spread and escalate among learners as disengagement becomes non-compliance and non-compliance becomes self-reinforcing.

Challenging behaviour

There's only really one example of challenging behaviour that's highlighted in this teacher's account, and that's when the learner objects to having to raise his hand to answer a question. Interestingly, the teacher describes this as *my own fault*. This is probably because he realises that he created this confrontation by issuing a direct order. A direct order can be refused, and this creates the risk of escalation. You'll have noticed that the teacher steps out of the confrontation by a quick change of activity. He doesn't feed it by arguing. He doesn't provide the learner with a platform from which to voice all his objections and complaints. He simply implements a complete change of activity, which draws everyone's immediate attention away from the incident. However, the damage has been done. This, like every drama or near-drama, has unsettled the class. We see the mixed table neglecting their task, turning their attention instead to a possible re-match, watching warily for signs of another biff between that learner and the teacher. When the teacher introduces another quick activity change, it's a discussion about rules. He knows – and is probably kicking himself for not remembering earlier – that negotiating rules is more productive than issuing orders. And we see it begin to work. The learners engage with the discussion; they comply with what's asked of them, probably because they now feel some ownership of it; and we see no recurrence of that challenging behaviour.

Critical Thinking Activity 3

» *Let's just rewind to the point where the teacher sees the learners on the all-male table writing something on the comic strip that he decides to ignore. He doesn't tell us what they were writing, but we can take a guess that it was something they shouldn't. Should we class this as challenging behaviour? Was he right to ignore it, do you think? What might have been his reasons for doing so? If he had responded to this provocation, what do you think would have been the consequences?*

» *We could argue that the way learners' disengagement manifests itself in this account seems to conform to the sort of behaviour typical of gender stereotypes. The males are noisy, disruptive, challenging; the girls are quiet and passive in their non-compliance. In your own experience of FE have you ever found this to be the case? How might such stereotypical notions, where they exist, affect teacher expectations and teaching styles?*

Typical classroom behaviour?

Recent research carried out into the behaviour of 16–19-year-old learners in FE colleges identified the most commonly occurring examples of disengagement and non-compliance

(Wallace, 2013). In 183 teaching sessions across several FE centres, the following were the most frequently observed signs of learner disengagement.

- Arriving late for the lesson.

- Talking at inappropriate times, either while the teacher is speaking or instead of concentrating on a task, thereby presenting a barrier to other students' learning.

- Using phones during class. This included making and receiving calls, messaging, accessing the internet and playing games.

- Rude, disrespectful or confrontational behaviour, either towards the teacher or towards other learners in the class.

- Failure to complete work or to submit it for an agreed deadline.

To anyone familiar with FE, this list will appear fairly predictable. There are no real surprises here. An important thing to note, however, is that none of these behaviours constitutes what we might consider serious, violent or aggressive behaviour. They are all fairly low key. But, although they may not exactly make for headline material, they still must give the teacher cause for concern because they create barriers to learning, both for the person concerned and for others who are more motivated. Also worth noting is that these same five examples of disengagement were observed in 16–19-year-old learners across all vocational areas and at all levels of qualification.

So what does this tell us? Well, one thing it suggests is that the disengaged behaviour or lack of motivation to learn is not to do with something that individual teachers are doing wrong. Rather, it suggests that it is something common to this age group in this sector. In that sense it could be taken as evidence to support some of the arguments we explored in Chapters 2 and 3 that put the case for young learners' motivation being undermined by their lack of choice or by the way the whole education and training system currently operates. Further evidence suggesting that these disengaged behaviours are not the fault of inexperienced, unqualified or incompetent teaching is that there was no correlation found between how frequently these sort of learner behaviours occurred and the age or gender or level of teaching qualification or length of professional experience of their teacher. Neither was there any correlation between the vocational area or subject being taught and these behaviours. Of course, this is only one small research project, but its findings add to the existing debate about how we can best support the learning of young people in FE. It reinforces the argument against adopting a deficit model of the teacher or the learner and looking instead at wider issues within the system itself.

All of those 'top five' behaviours show, to a greater or lesser extent, a lack of respect – for the teacher, the college, the learner's peers and for themselves. As this is a chapter about respect, we need to unpack this idea a little more. Being a teacher doesn't automatically gain you respect; and respect is not something that can be demanded. It has to be earned. Most experienced teachers will tell you that the best way to establish a culture of respect in your classes is to model the behaviour you wish to encourage. Demonstrate respect for your learners and they are more likely to show respect for you – and for each other. Certainly, research tells us that some learners in FE find the mutually respectful teacher–learner relationship boosts their confidence to actively engage with their learning in a way they felt unable to do at school (for example, Fuller and Macfadyen, 2012; Peart, 2012). A teacher who habitually shouts at learners or belittles them or behaves contemptuously towards them may foster an atmosphere of fear where learners think twice about stepping out of line. But this is not the same thing as respect. In the scenario we've just looked at it's probably no coincidence that what triggers the outburst of confrontational behaviour is the teacher unthinkingly demanding that people with answers raise their hands. This is too much like school for one learner at least. He's in FE now and wants to be accorded the respect he feels is due to him as an adult. On the other hand, being given the opportunity to negotiate their own rules seems to be taken by the learners as a mark of respect, and consequently they seem reasonably happy to co-operate.

Respect, rules, razzmatazz and rewards

We can identify *respect* as one of four key motivators that teachers can use to encourage 16–19-year-olds to engage with their learning in FE. The other three are having clear *rules*; injecting some *razzmatazz*, or fun, into the lesson; and using *rewards* – whether it's praise or prizes (Wallace, 2007). We can see Dan using all of these in the lesson he describes to us. In fact, you might find it interesting to go back and see if you can pick these instances out.

The same research that identified the five most frequent indicators of disengagement, also looked for data to show what strategies teachers used to effectively address these. No clear evidence emerged about what lines of action worked and what didn't; but what did emerge was something of central relevance to our discussion in this chapter. The observation reports indicated that learner motivation and positive behaviour were at their best in classes where there appeared to be a positive, cheerful and mutually respectful relationship between teacher and learners (Wallace, 2013). Can we call this a strategy? Probably not. It seems to be more about relationship and respect; about the overall attitude of the teacher rather than about something that can be included in a lesson plan. This echoes very closely the contention of educational pioneers such as Knowles (1913–97) and Freire (1921–97) who argued for a teacher–learner relationship based on support and mutual respect rather than on power and authority. And it also seems to reflect the ideas of humanist theorists such as Abraham Maslow (1908–70) and Carl Rogers (1902–87), who argue that learners' basic human needs, such as the need for acceptance and a sense of belonging, must be met before they can engage with the business of learning.

Critical Thinking Activity 4

Here is another teacher's account of a classroom experience. Drawing on what you have learnt in this chapter so far, identify the behaviours she is observing, and consider the following:

» *What does she do to successfully address some of the problems?*

» *Does she herself cause any escalation?*

» *Is there anything she could have done differently?*

» *How do the following come into her behaviour management strategy: respect, razzmatazz, rules, reward?*

» *In what ways does she set a good example for her learners by demonstrating respect?*

CASE STUDY

Corrie

My name's Corrie and I'm in the final term of my teaching qualification. So far I've done about 60 hours teaching this year, not counting team teaching and observations. My subject is performing arts, and one of the things I've noticed since I started here is that a lot of youngsters seem to have opted for it because they think somehow it's 'easy'. And then they find out it's not, and that there's writing to do and theory to learn, and at that point they sort of close down. So the hardest part of my job so far has been trying to get them back on board and trying to show them that they can do it, if they're just prepared to put a bit of effort in. Anyway, this morning was a typical session. We started with a warm-up workout. They like the loud music and it sort of gets some energy going. I stand with my back to them so they can copy exactly what I'm doing – right arm, left leg and so on. The trouble with this is that I can't see very well what's going on. There's a long mirror down one wall of the studio and I can keep my eye on most of them in that. But there are one or two blind spots, and the lazy ones know exactly where those are. So when I'd got them into the routine and they'd got the moves, I let them carry on while I turned around to take a look. In one of the blind spots over in the corner was Jessi who's very overweight. She was just jigging about on the spot, minimal movement. And on the other side were two of the lads doing something with a phone. When they all saw I'd turned round they pretended they'd been joining in but it was obvious they didn't know the moves. And I'd had about enough of those three, always the ones to opt out. So I stopped the music – loads of groans – and asked Jessi what she was doing. She said she'd just been taking a break because she was out of breath. Well, the thing is I know better than to mention her weight – that would be seen as offensive. But I know she smokes. She's always going out for toilet breaks and coming back smelling of cigs. So I said to her, Well, Jessi, if you're out of breath it's your own fault. You need to do something about it. I meant the smoking. But she thought it was a poke at her weight and just went off on one, screaming and shouting at me, telling me I'd got no respect and she wasn't going to stay around and be disrespected etc., etc. And then she stomped off. And at that point two other girls, who are normally really good, started telling me off, telling me I'd been rude and I should think about people's feelings. I felt a complete loser. I was really glad my mentor wasn't observing. I'd have been mortified. And while I'm being 'told off', all the rest of the group are standing around like an audience, probably thinking this was the best bit of the performing arts course yet! One of the most difficult bits of this for me is that there were those two other students who'd not been joining in either, but looked like they were going to get away with it because I couldn't suddenly turn on them before I'd managed this crisis and established some calm.

The worst thing I could have done, I think, would be to enter into a shouting match with the girls who were haranguing me. So I said nothing, but kept steady eye contact with them until they'd finished. And then I said, OK. Now let me tell you what really happened. I was advising her to give up smoking – same advice I'd give to any of you who I knew had the habit. Because in this line of work you've got to be fit enough to take the strain. It's an incredibly tough business to be in. And if you can't keep up with a warm-up routine at age 16 you need to do something about it. Jessi misunderstood what I was saying. Perhaps that's because she's worried about her weight and it's on her mind. But right now, if you're concerned about her, the important thing is for one of you to go and see if she's OK. Explain what I was saying. And see if *you* can get her throw those cigs away. *And then, because they were all listening and I could see I was getting through to them, I said,* And I can see you're embarrassed, but don't be. Apologies accepted. OK?

So one of her 'defenders' – who actually I don't think had ever been particularly friendly with her – went off on that mission to find her. And I got the rest of them back doing the warm-up, with the music turned up loud, and I went over to the two lads for a quiet word. Phones off. Join in the warm-up. They've both got potential, so don't throw it away. All that sort of thing. The music was up and the rest of the group was occupied, so this wasn't a conversation held in public. But if there's one thing I've learnt these past few months it's to not let learners get away with non-participation. It's bad for the morale of the rest. And sometimes the ones shirking it just need a bit of encouragement. Sometimes it's all about them feeling self-conscious, not wanting to look stupid, just not having enough confidence in themselves. It goes with the age, really. And all they need, usually, is a bit of cheering on. But if you let it go, it just gets worse, and has a knock-on effect, and that's not fair to any of them.

Writing up this journal has made me reflect a bit more on what happened with Jessi. Maybe it wasn't just the cigs. Maybe she feels stupid doing those routines, carrying all that weight. Maybe I was reading her wrong. Because it would explain why she was so ready to fly off the handle and assume I was criticising her weight. Sometimes when there's a behaviour problem, it's actually a learner telling you something through their behaviour that they wouldn't want, or be able, to say out loud in words. I'm thinking now I probably handled that incident with her all wrong. I need to have a think, and maybe some one-to-one tutorial time with her.

Looking beyond the surface: reading and interpreting learner behaviour

We discussed some of the systemic reasons for learner disengagement in Chapters 2 and 3. Here we see a teacher drawing our attention to the equally important individual and personal reasons that learners may have for withdrawing from active participation in their learning. What she is saying here is that non-compliance or lack of motivation can be seen as a signal that all is not well. Yes, it may be an indicator of socio-economic trends and youth unemployment. But it may also be an unintentional message from the learner that they need your help. A learner may refuse to attempt a task because they fear it's beyond them, or because they fear ridicule from others in the group for being compliant to the teacher's wishes. Or a learner may opt out of making any effort because they find the task too easy and therefore boring; or because others in the group won't bother pulling their weight and so why should they. What looks like simply lack of respect may be a signal that something more complex needs addressing in terms of the learner's needs. If we see behaviour as a way of communicating, we're more likely to take the time to consider what it's telling us.

Chapter reflections

In this chapter we have explored the relevance of respect in FE teaching. We have looked in particular at:

» *how respect became part of the education and training agenda;*

» *what we mean by respect and whether it's about behaviour or attitude, or both;*

» *why it is considered a teacher's responsibility to encourage respect;*

» *what teachers can do to encourage respect;*

» *the difference between disengagement, non-compliance and challenging behaviour;*

» *what recent research tells us about learner behaviour in FE;*

» *strategies teachers use: respect, rules, razzmatazz and rewards;*

» *how learners' behaviour may be telling us something we need to hear.*

Taking it further

If you would like to read more about practical strategies for encouraging respect and learner engagement, you may enjoy the following book, which provides plenty of advice linked to lively accounts of FE teachers' experiences.

Wallace, S. (2007) *Getting the Buggers Motivated in FE*. London: Continuum.

You might also find it interesting to read the full text of Callaghan's 1974 Ruskin College speech, which you can find at www.education.guardian/thegreatdebate

References

Fuller, C. and Macfadyen, T. (2012) 'What, with your grades?' Students' Motivations and Experiences of Vocational Courses in Further Education. *Journal of Vocational Education and Training*, 64(1): 87–101.

Peart, S. (2012) The Impact of Culture on Participation: Black Men and Boys' Experience of Further Education. *Race Equality Teaching*, 3: 7–9.

Wallace, S. (2007) *Getting the Buggers Motivated in FE*. London: Continuum.

Wallace, S. (2013) When You're Smiling: Exploring How Teachers Motivate and Engage Learners in the Further Education Sector. *Journal of Further and Higher Education*,

9 Letters from the front: insider discourse

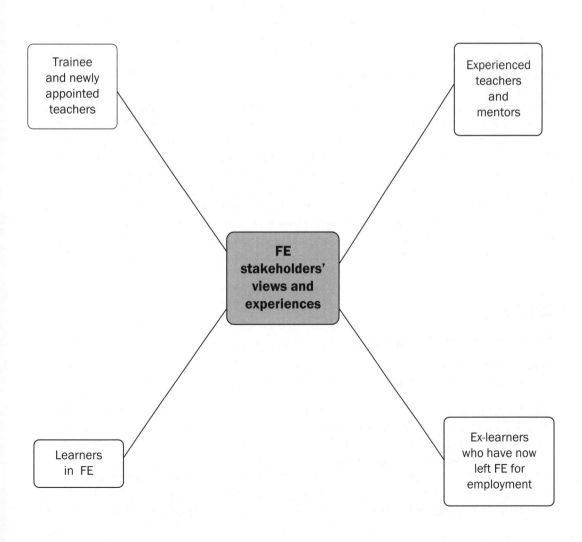

Chapter aims

This chapter is designed to help you gain an understanding of:

* the ways in which some of the issues discussed in this book so far are perceived in the day-to-day experience of trainee teachers, newly qualified teachers, experienced teachers, new learners and learners who have now progressed from FE to employment;

* the impact some of these issues have on their roles, activities and expectations;

* how the same developments and policies can have different implications for different stakeholders;

* the range of positive action that can be taken by teachers to address difficult issues.

Introduction

In this chapter we're going to explore some of the themes and ideas discussed so far through the views and experiences of key groups within FE. It's an insider's view; and it will help us to understand how these policies and arguments impact on the lived experience of learners and those who support their learning. It will give us a practical perspective on some of the theoretical arguments we've encountered, and will provide a clear context in which to consider a range of positive responses. The chapter includes a series of conversations with pairs of individuals from key stakeholder groups. This doesn't include employers for the simple reason that the focus is on the lived experienced of learning and working inside the FE system. In each encounter the researcher asks an initial question or two to get things going, and then sits back so that we can listen to the dialogue that follows between the two participants. This approach could be seen as a combination of interview and mini focus group. After each conversation you will find an activity that will encourage you to think critically and analytically about what has been said, and to consider how it relates to the content of previous chapters. You'll find the conversations with learners come last. This is not because they are the least important. On the contrary, it's to ensure that they have the last word. We'll begin, however, with two trainee teachers who are working towards their professional qualification.

CASE STUDY

The trainee teachers' perspective

Researcher: So you've both had a few weeks now working in an FE college, and I wanted to ask you: what were your first impressions? Was it how you expected it to be?

TT1: It's been fantastic! I don't think I knew what to expect, really. I'd never been inside an FE college before – can you believe it?! I didn't even know anybody who'd been in FE. I did A levels at school and went to uni and then worked in a charitable trust for four years. And part of that was advising people with literacy problems. And I thought, you know, hey, I'm quite good at this. I enjoy this. And that was when I decided to be a teacher. And obviously FE was where I could make the most difference, right? And it's been amazing. The people I work with are so nice. They're so dedicated. And I'm just starting to get that buzz, you know?

Where I can see I'm actually helping people to learn and making a difference to their lives. Do you know what I mean?

TT2: *Yeah, sort of. I mean, it's a bit different for me. I came through the FE system as a learner. I never did very well at school and I couldn't get a place in the sixth form – wouldn't have wanted it anyway. And I went to my local college because I couldn't think of anything else to do, really. It was just sort of go with the flow. But it changed my view of education completely. It was like suddenly waking up and thinking, Oh yeah. I'm quite bright actually. And I find learning about stuff quite interesting. And I want to learn more. I just sort of took off. I loved it. The teachers talked to us like we were adults. You could have a laugh with them. They made me see I'd got some potential. And this was after years in school thinking of myself as a loser. I mean, eventually I did the first year of my degree at college and then went on to university. And what brought me into teaching really was this feeling that I wanted to put something back, you know what I mean? College had turned my life around and it had shown me what good teaching looked like, and I just wanted to pass some of that on. I want to be as good a teacher as those that helped me. And I want to make that difference to kids' lives – same as happened to mine. Show them they're not thick. Give them their confidence back. Help them to feel as good about themselves as they deserve to.*

TT1: *Yeah, that's it. I mean, I know I didn't come to it like that, but I can see how some of the learners here straight from school have just got the idea that they're failures. And they're not. It's the system that's failed. It's failed to recognise what they've got to offer and it's failed to engage their interest and it's failed to – well basically it's left them with no confidence. No self-respect. They leave school feeling crap about themselves, don't they? Not all of them. I mean it's not all of them, by any means. But it's enough of them to make you see that there's something wrong somewhere. I mean, I was quite shocked at first by some of the behaviour. You know, like I'd be observing an experienced teacher and what I'd be seeing was this complete lack of, well, this lack of interest really.*

TT2: *What, the teacher?*

TT1: *No! God, no. The learners. Just not interested. So how's that happened? The teachers – well, I've not met one yet who isn't completely dedicated to what they're doing. There's some brilliant teachers. So why don't some of these kids want to listen? And then it began to dawn on me: they probably think they're going to fail anyway, so they're thinking why should they bother, you know? And you can see the teachers doing all sorts to try and build the learners' confidence...*

TT2: *I don't think it's just a confidence thing, though. I mean, thinking about my own experience as a student in FE, I think some of them feel a bit trapped. They've come into FE because they can't see anywhere else to go. Like me. That's how I was. And it makes you mad, you know? Resentful. And they get here and there's some others who feel the same way, and it sort of sets up a culture of resistance. Not just disengagement, but actual resistance. You know. Why should I do any work? What am I ever going to get out of it? That sort of thing.*

TT1: *That's one of things that was such a culture shock to me. But it's a challenge, isn't it? It makes you really think hard about what you're doing and why. Lesson planning, you know.*

Like, how am I going to get this lot interested? How can I get this bit of the curriculum over to them in some way that doesn't involve me just standing and talking at them? Where's the hook? What can I put in there to catch their interest? All that. And the other challenge, I think, is to learn to read the learners' behaviour. Like, I started off the first couple of days thinking it must be personal. It must be because they didn't like the teacher. And then you realise it's not. It's actually about how they're feeling. The learner, I mean. They're sort of saying, I don't think I can do this. Or I'm scared. Or My mates'll laugh at me if I look too interested. *You know. And once you realise that, it all sort of falls into place, what you need to do, how you can best support them.*

TT2: *Yeah, that's right. Because what you realise is that the whole thing isn't about you, the teacher. It's about them, the learners. And once you stop thinking about what's going on in your own head, and turn your attention to what's going on in theirs I reckon you've cracked it.*

TT1: *That's right. Because there's a temptation to see this teacher training as being about teacher performance – you know, all about what you* do *and how you do it. And that can distract you from the real focus, which is the needs of the learners.*

TT2: *That's probably inevitable with standards-based training, right?*

TT1: *Probably, yeah.*

Critical Thinking Activity 1

Now consider the following questions. Take some time to read the conversation again if you need to. You may find it useful to write your answers down and to compare them or discuss them with a mentor or colleague.

» *What themes discussed in previous chapters are being touched on here?*

» *What contribution does this argument make to the debate about* parity of esteem?

» *What new points, if any, are raised?*

» *What can you learn from this conversation that you could usefully apply in your practice?*

» *The trainee teachers each present their own reason for wanting to become an FE teacher. What would say are your own reasons, and do they coincide in any way with either of theirs?*

CASE STUDY

Listening to newly qualified teachers

Interviewer: *You're both coming to the end of your first year as qualified teachers in FE. Can you tell me a bit about what that experience has been like for you?*

T1: Exhausting! [Laughs] I'm completely knackered. And sometimes I've wondered whether I was going to keep all the plates spinning. But it's been so rewarding, it so has. I teach mainly the younger learners, 16- and 17-year-olds but also some 14–16-year-olds, and they change so much in a year. You see such a difference. I don't think you see that when you're a trainee teacher because then you're mostly borrowing other people's classes, or you have someone sitting in with you and it's not quite the same. But having a group and seeing them through the year and watching them develop skills and understanding, and seeing them become more adult. It's been really good. Really satisfying. I can't imagine any other job that would make me feel I was doing this much good.

T2: Really? I mean, I've had some really great moments, too. But I've also had some terrible moments. You know, learners playing up, whatever I do. An inspector watching me trying to get a group of girls to look even mildly interested – with absolutely no success. Learners in my classes who actively wanted to be doing something else entirely. A section head who's checked all my marking all year just because I'm new. [Laughs] It's been a complete roller-coaster. You know, some of it really exhilarating like you say; but some of it bloody horrible.

T1: Yeah but that's life, innit? That's how it'd be in any job. Good days, bad days. It's never all going to be rosy, is it? It's never all going to be easy. That's not what we're in it for. We know it's a struggle sometimes. We know it's a challenge. That's what makes it feel so good when we can see we're making a difference. You know? I've had some bad days as well, but on balance…

T2: Yeah, I know. I'm not saying it's bad or I regret it or anything like that. What I'm saying is it's not easy. You get your qualification and you think, Right. I'm qualified now. I can do this. *But then a couple of weeks in you start to realise that there's so much stuff you just haven't covered. There's so much stuff you just have to learn by being there and doing it. Reflecting on what's worked and what's not worked, and then going back to the drawing board and re-thinking and re-planning. I think the standards are useful for the sort of basic practical stuff – lesson planning and turning learning outcomes into learner activities you can assess – all that sort of thing. But they don't cover the relationship things, the affective stuff, the empathy – all the things you need if you're going to build up mutual respect. They look as if they do. But because they have to be written in an instrumental, observable sort of way, they can't really help you with things like recognising the importance of relationships, emotional intelligence, you know? I think I was lucky because I had a very good mentor last year at my teaching practice college and she really helped with all that. But the mentor this college has given me for this year is rubbish. I'm sorry, but he is. I can never get hold of him…*

T1: Hang on, I just want to go back to what you were saying about the standards. Because you said something about re-thinking, you know, in the light of something that's happened. Going back and thinking again about your planning. And I reckon the main thing that's really struck me this year is that teacher training needs to be much more about reflection. If you're really reflecting on what you do, and whether it's worked, and if not why not, and all that, then you're more likely to do a good job than if you just stick to a set way of doing stuff – you know, competent in this, competent in that – a 'one size fits all' approach. Because I think that's what standards end up being really. It's inevitable, isn't it? And there isn't one right way of doing things in teaching. It's an art, isn't it – not a science. I don't know who said that but it's true. If a tutor or mentor observes me facilitating a group discussion and then ticks that off, you know, like, Yep. She can do that. She's attained the required standard on that, and then I have a group where every aspect of the way I did it last time wouldn't work at all, and I know it – well, it's crazy isn't it? What we ought to be assessed on is our willingness and ability to reflect and adapt and to respond to our learners as individuals. And that's ongoing. You can't observe someone a couple of times and say, Yeah. That's fine. They can do that. Tick. You know?

T2: I completely agree. But what I was saying, right, was that your mentor is really important. Your mentor can help you with all that. And if you get a rubbish one, you're screwed.

Critical Thinking Activity 2

When you've looked at the following questions, you may want to read the conversation again before considering your answers. You may find it useful to write your answers down and to compare them or discuss them with a mentor or colleague.

» *What themes discussed in previous chapters are being touched on here?*

» *What contribution does this argument make to the debate about a) standards for teachers; and b) FE teachers' role and status?*

» *What new points, if any, are raised?*

» *What can you learn from this conversation that you could usefully apply in your practice?*

» *The teachers argue vigorously for the importance of reflective practice. Can you identify a recent occasion when you have made changes to your planning or practice as a result of reflection on a specific experience or incident?*

CASE STUDY

What experienced teachers have to say

Interviewer: OK. Thank you for sparing the time to talk about your professional experiences. I understand you've both been teaching in FE for several years now. One of you for over 20 years, I believe?

ET1: *Yes, that's me. Twenty-three years. I started in 1991, just before everything changed with Incorporation and that.*

ET2: *What was that like?*

ET1: *Oh well, that was long time ago. I still had hair then. [Laughs] No, it was a strange time. I mean, I'd only been in the job a year, so from my point of view it wasn't such an upheaval* *as it was for some of the people who'd been in the business for years. I think the main thing that troubled everyone at the time was the change in the conditions of service – losing the long holidays and working longer hours with bigger classes for the same money. I don't think it was political or social implications that were of immediate concern. That only hit people afterwards.*

ET2*: Such as?*

ET1*: Well, the whole thing about the competitive market for a start. Because there were sud-denly training organisations springing up everywhere and competing with colleges for the same funding budget. So there was this constant sense of uncertainty – would we still be in business this time next year? Would we still have a job? There were college closures and mergers going on all over the place. The thing was that suddenly colleges were responsible fully for keeping things afloat financially, and often there just wasn't expertise. Everyone had started out as a teacher, not in financial management. And we were competing with schools as well by then. So there was this sudden shift towards a business model and away from the idea of providing a service. It was the start of education and training as a commodity, really, when you look back on it. Measuring outcomes in financial terms rather than in terms of the difference they made to people's lives. But you work with what you've got, don't you? Times change, and you have to change with the times. Maybe the biggest difference is that when I started out, there were still jobs for school leavers, and kids were still turning to FE as a con-scious choice, with an eye to the career they wanted to follow. It's not quite like that now.*

ET2*: I think that's true. I mean, I've only been teaching in FE for eight years, so I don't have that same scale of comparison. But I think it's true that a lot of kids today come into FE almost by accident. Their choices are pretty limited. A lot of them would like to be doing something else, but didn't quite make it. GCSE results not good enough, or they had unreal-istic ambitions like being a celebrity or something. So for them FE is always going to be second-best. And that makes it very hard on the teacher. You know, you love your subject and you go bounding into the workshop, full of enthusiasm, and you know right from the start that there's going to be at least one or two learners there who just aren't interested. They've absolutely no ambition to qualify or succeed in your subject. And it has an impact, inevitably, on the rest. I don't mean it's catching, necessarily. What I mean is that you spend a disproportionate amount of your time trying to get these learners onside – and the others get less of your time. And you know that's not fair. So it feels stressful. And also it has a big impact on your lesson planning and style of teaching. You're thinking all the time,* How can I encourage these two? How can I draw them in and get them excited about the subject? *And you're ignoring the learning needs of the others, aren't you. It's an impossible dilemma, really. The last college I was teaching at wasn't so bad. They did a lot of counselling and advice before allocating places on different programmes, so that at least there was some sort of fit between learners' interests and the course they ended up on. They don't have that here. It sometimes looks like a bit of a 'bums on seats policy'. You know,* We're low on numbers for the level 2 building and construction and so we'll guide a few more on to there. *Whether they're interested or not, basically. It's what I'd call solving one problem by creating another, bigger one. But it bears out what you were saying about things being finance-led rather than people-led, I think.*

ET1: Yes, I think everything you're saying is true. I've only ever worked at this college, so I can't speak for anywhere else. But I'd guess it's pretty much the same everywhere. In a competitive market some of these things are inevitable. But I like that idea of your old college trying to get a better fit between learners and courses, to minimise the numbers of kids who just switch off. Maybe you should suggest it to the principal. Tell him it's like a Sorting Hat. He's always fancied himself as Dumbledore. [Laughs]

Critical Thinking Activity 3

Read the following questions carefully and take some time to consider your answers. You may find it useful to write your answers down and to compare them or discuss them with a mentor or colleague.

» *What themes discussed in previous chapters do you recognise in these teachers' conversation?*

» *What contribution do these teachers make to the debate about a) learner choice; and b) the advantages and disadvantages of a competitive market in education and training?*

» *Do they raise any points that you had not previously considered?*

» *What is your view of Teacher 2's argument about the negative impact of disengaged learners on the rest of the class? Do you agree with the points she makes? Drawing on your own experience, are there any you would add?*

CASE STUDY

Listening to learners new to the sector

Researcher: You're both about halfway through your first term in FE. What's it been like for you so far?

L1: *Epic. Not like school. They treat you like an adult here. Yeah. It's alright.*

Researcher: *What about you?*

L2: *It's alright. Yeah.*

Researcher: *Just alright?*

L2: *Yeah. It's OK. Teachers are OK and that. But it's a bit boring.*

Researcher: *Boring how?*

L2: *It's just not interesting, is it? It's not about what I'm interested in and that. It's better than school, yeah. At least they don't make you feel stupid and that. But I'm not interested in electrics. I never wanted to do that. I wanted to do computer studies. That was the only thing I enjoyed at school, computer studies. So why would I want to come here and do electrics* and that? It's boring. What's the point? I'm never going to do it for a job, am I? So why would I be arsed to do assignments and that? And turn up for the early session? I'm not going to do that, am I? The teachers are alright. Well, most of them. I feel sorry for them, really. They're stuck with me and I'm not the only one. Don't get me wrong, I don't kick off or nowt but there's whole lessons sometimes when I'm just taking the piss and the teacher's like, Come on, Keanu. You can do this. It's your own time you're wasting. *And this and that. And I'm like,* Yeah, yeah. Whatever.

L1: *Was you like that at school? That was what I was like at school. But it's different here, you get me? It's like you've stayed the same, sounds like to me. Like this place is different from school but you've just stayed the same. That's what it sounds like to me.*

L2: *Maybe. But maybe you're doing what you want. I'm not doing what I want, am I? If I was doing what I want I wouldn't be bored and that, would I?*

L1: *So why you not doing what you want, then? Why you not doing computers and that if that's what you want to do? How come?*

L2: *I couldn't get on it, could I? They only have this number of places and they didn't have one for me. They gave them to people with grade C and above in IT, which I didn't have. So they said,* Hard luck. You're going to do electrics. *[Laughs]*

L1: *But if you didn't want to do it, why are you at college at all?*

L2: *Where else am I going to be, man? Running Microsoft? It's college or NEET, innit?*

L1: Right. I'm lucky then. I wanted to do business studies and that's what I'm doing. And it's epic. The teachers are like really friendly and that. And they don't order you about. They discuss stuff with you and you get to make your own decisions, you get me? And like we do everything in this Practice Office, so it's like a proper work environment so we get used to it. And if you're late it's treated like you're late for your job and you get a warning. And we have teams and you move from one to the next so that you get experience in all of them. There's like the creatives and the sales team and accounts and all this and that. And it's like you suddenly jump from being treated like a kid who's not good at anything to being an adult who gets treated with respect. I did rubbish at school. It feels like I've been really lucky to get on this course. And if I took my school exams again I bet I'd do really well this time because I know now I'm a winner, but when I was in school I just thought I was a loser.

Critical Thinking Activity 4

The following questions are designed to help you to analyse this conversation between learners. Read them carefully and take some time to consider your answers. You may find it useful to write your answers down and to compare them or discuss them with a mentor or colleague.

» *These two learners report very different experiences of FE. What would you identify as the underlying reasons for this; and how does it relate to some of the debates we've explored in earlier chapters?*

> » Does anything either of them says surprise you? If so, what?

> » Is there any correspondence between what they each have to say, and the points raised by the experienced teachers in the previous section?

> » Have you learnt anything from this conversation that you could use to inform your own professional practice?

CASE STUDY

The view of learners who have now progressed to employment

Interviewer: Both of you attended the local FE college at one time, I think?

EL1: Yes, I finished there just last year.

EL2: I've been qualified and employed for three years now. Yeah.

Interviewer: So what was FE like for you?

EL2: It was the making of me, really. I went in there as a bolshie, leery 16-year-old, thinking college was a complete waste of time, and I came out four years later with a good qualification that got me a good job. And I was a different person. It's difficult to say exactly what it was that turned me around. Part of it was simply growing up, obviously – and that would have happened anyway. But I think a big part of it was about the people. The teachers – I was really lucky with my teachers. Maybe they're all like that – I don't know. But they wouldn't play my game. Do you know what I mean? They wouldn't play the angry teacher game. They were wise to what I was like. They drew a line, but they wouldn't shout, wouldn't spend time getting mad at me. In the end I got it, you know. I got what I should've learnt long before that, which was that you can get the teacher's attention by getting on with the work. And it's a much better feeling, that kind of attention. Approval. I'd not had approval before. And when I worked out that was the way to get it, there was no stopping me. But it wasn't just that those teachers had real skill. It was that they were people I wanted to approve of me, you know? The way they were – confident and friendly and that. And respectful. All the teachers I had knew how to listen like what you had to say was worth listening to. I'd never had that before either.

EL1: I think school teachers can be like that. I had some good ones when I was at school. But you're still a child there, aren't you? The thing about getting into FE is that it's an adult world. There's always some dickheads wanting to spoil it...

EL2: Yeah, that was me. [Laughs]

EL1: But I think most of the people in my group responded to the environment by trying to behave more like adults. If you're treated like one you're more likely to behave like one, yeah? They can't do that in school because you're still kids. And also you don't have much choice about being there. But if you're in FE it's because you want to be. That makes a difference.

EL2: I don't think that's true though, not for everybody. I think some people end up in college because there's nowhere else to go. And that was me, to be honest. It's not where I'd have chosen to be. Not to start with. And if I hadn't had the teachers I had, I might have kept that attitude all the way through and wasted my time and everybody else's.

EL1: Yeah, I think that's right about teachers. I think that's the thing that makes the difference. Good teachers. And you wonder sometimes whether they realise the difference they make. I don't think I ever told mine what they'd done for me. Did you?

EL2: No. Well, you'd be embarrassed like, wouldn't you? And they probably would as well.

Researcher: I think any teacher would be really pleased to be told they'd made a difference. There's lots of very dedicated teachers out there, and I don't think that's always appreciated.

EL2: No. You're right. But you don't think of that when you're young, do you? You just take it for granted that they know. You've made me think now. I might go back and see them – tell them how I'm getting on.

EL1: The other thing that people don't often talk about is the stuff they teach you that's not just about work. How to behave with other people. How to watch your language. How to think about what you're doing before you do it, and about what sort of a job you made of it after it's done.

EL2: Skills for life.

EL1: Skills for life, yeah. Not just work. Because, let's face it, any of us could be out of work tomorrow the way things are going. And if all your skills are to do with work, where does that leave you? But things I learnt from my teachers were like how to keep cool when you're feeling mad. How to relate to people...

EL2: Resilience. That's something one of my old teachers taught me. And none of that stuff is officially in the lessons, like. It's the learning that happens between the cracks that's sometimes the really important stuff. You realise that later on. And that's what you get with good teachers.

Critical Thinking Activity 5

Read through the following questions and consider your answers carefully. If you write your answers down you'll find this makes it easier to compare them or discuss them with a mentor or colleague.

» *What do we learn from this conversation about the role of teachers in FE?*

» *Did anything that was said surprise you?*

» *In what ways does the conversation reflect some of the debates we've explored in earlier chapters?*

» *Is there anything you would take from this conversation in order to inform your own professional practice? If so, what? And why?*

Chapter reflections

In this chapter we've listened to FE insiders discuss their experiences, values and beliefs. We've heard from trainee teachers, early career teachers, experienced teachers, new learners and learners who have successfully completed their college course. Some of the themes that have emerged relate closely to debates we've considered in earlier chapters. These include:

» *the role of the FE teacher;*

» *what makes a good teacher;*

» *professional standards for teachers;*

» *the issues of learner choice;*

» *learner behaviour and motivation;*

» *the impact of a market ideology on FE provision;*

» *the vocational curriculum.*

Taking it further

One of the experienced teachers being interviewed tells us about the impact on FE of entering a competitive market in the 1990s. For a critical and lively look at market ideology you could read:

Sandel, M.J. (2013) *What Money Can't Buy: The Moral Limits of Markets*. London: Penguin.

Some other useful further reading you could do for this chapter would be to go back and look through earlier chapters to remind yourself of the historical or ideological arguments that lie behind the points of view these people have been expressing in their interviews. In this way you can make the link between theory and how it is applied or experienced in practice.

References

There are no references to literature because none of the people involved in these conversations cited any.

10 Conclusions and applications

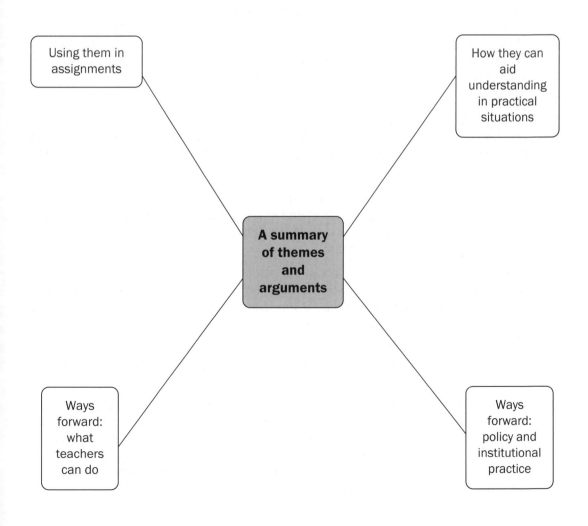

Chapter aims

This chapter offers:

- a summary of the main themes we've encountered in this book;

- some examples of how you might draw on your knowledge of these to gain a better understanding of incidents and situations that arise in your professional practice;

- some examples of ways in which you might draw on these to provide context and detail in written assignments, both for initial teacher training and for CPD up to Masters level;

- a discussion about ways forward, both at a practical level for individual teachers and managers, and also at a policy level for the sector as a whole.

Summaries of themes and arguments

We've encountered a number of recurring themes in this book. Some, such as the questions of parity and choice, have threaded through every chapter. All, from the social origins of FE to the debate over the vocational curriculum, throw light on our everyday experiences and practices and help us to better understand them. None of this is empty theory. Far from it. We can utilise this knowledge and understanding in our day-to-day teaching, as well as in our formal professional development, to enhance our reflective practice and better support our students' and trainees' learning.

There are several ways in which we could divide up the themes of this book. You may have identified themes and arguments that are not listed here. This doesn't mean they're not 'important'. Make a note of them and keep them in mind in the later sections of this chapter. The main themes as I see them are:

- *The status of FE.* This is concerned with the way in which its origins are associated with certain ideas about class and status, and how these have become self-perpetuating, reflected and reinforced by popular culture. This is perhaps the major theme that in many ways underlies all the others.

- *Recruitment and choice.* This is about the lack of real choice for some school leavers, who enter FE unwillingly or with the sense that they are settling for second-best. This is one of the explanations offered for the lack of engagement apparent in colleges among some 16–19-year-olds.

- *Disengagement and negative behaviour.* This is a theme in itself. Although it applies to only a minority of learners, the disengagement of a few can disrupt the learning of the many.

- *Teachers' role and responsibilities.* This theme includes the debate about professional standards for teachers in FE, and the use of the deficit model in relation to learner achievement. We've looked at the argument that poor achievement is not necessarily the fault of teachers, because there are wider, socio-economic issues that come into play; but that nevertheless teachers have responsibility to ensure learning takes place. This theme also encompasses questions about the status of FE teachers.

» Drawing on what we've discussed in earlier chapters, what do *you* think is going on?

» Based on what you have learnt from earlier chapters, how would you advise Miles to proceed?

CASE STUDY 2

Anni is a trainee teacher on her first placement in a large FE college. One of her first tasks is to observe an experienced teacher with one of the classes she will later be teaching herself. She arrives in the classroom before anyone else and takes a seat at the back. The learners begin arriving. The teacher, Vlad, enters with the last of them and begins setting up the data projector. This takes some time. The learners are talking among themselves. Vlad shouts at them at intervals to *Be quiet!* He doesn't look up from the equipment until he's ready to begin. Then he puts up the first slide and tells the learners, *Right. Copy that down.* Before some of them have finished he puts up the next slide and tells them to copy that down as well. The lesson progresses in this way. One learner puts up her hand, and Vlad tells her to put it down.

Get your hand down, Haylee. Just get on with it. To Anni this looks like sheer rudeness, and she begins to feel uncomfortable about what she's observing. At one point Vlad shouts at the learners again: *It's simple enough. Just copy it down. Even you lot can do this, surely!*

By the end of the lesson Anni is feeling very depressed, and also indignant on the learners' behalf. She speaks to Vlad as the two of them are leaving the room. *I'm not quite sure what I've seen,* she says to him. *I'm not sure what was going on there.*

Oh you just have to keep them out of trouble, says Vlad. *They're not good for much. They end up here because nowhere else will have them. All you can do is keep on top of them. They're not interested in learning.* Anni can't help thinking that she wouldn't be much interested in learning either if her experience of it had been like that. Later that day, still trying to make sense of what she's seen, she comes and talks it over with you.

» What background information would you be able to give Anni to help her to understand what's going on here and help her to contextualise it? Where does Vlad's view of these learners come from? How is it being perpetuated here?

» What would you advise her to do when she herself comes to teach this class? What will the learners need from her in order to engage properly with their learning?

CASE STUDY 3

You have volunteered to go and talk to Year 11 pupils in a local school about progression options into FE in general and the department you work for in particular. This is what's known in your college jargon as a 'recruitment presentation', and in the school jargon as 'career

- *The vocational curriculum*. This theme is a complex one, incorporating arguments about 'useful knowledge', instrumentalism and liberalism. It also includes the question of whether the instrumental nature of the vocational curriculum contributes to the causes of learner disengagement.

- *Policies and word games*. This is about how to read below the surface meaning of policy documents and identify the values and beliefs that drive them. It's about how the language we use about FE both reflects and reinforces dominant beliefs and ideologies.

It's possible to see a causal progression in these themes, one leading to another. The perceived status of the sector creating the issues with recruitment and choice, and those issues becoming an underlying cause of negative behaviour in learners, and so on. Or we could envisage an alternative 'sequence' presented as a flowchart.

What is clear is that all of these themes are interlinked in a complex way. And in the next section we're going to consider how we can draw on our understanding of this to help us to with our problem-solving in everyday practice.

Critical Thinking Activity 1

»   *Are there any themes which have emerged for you from your reading of this book that are not included in this list?*

»   *What additional links can you see between the themes? How could you represent this in chart form?*

Applying what we've learnt in practice

In this section we're going to look at three scenarios or case studies. After each one you'll be asked to consider which themes or arguments you could usefully draw on in order to understand what is going on and resolve the situation. You may find it useful to jot your answers down so that you can discuss your ideas with a colleague or mentor.

CASE STUDY 1

Miles is teaching a group of level 2 learners. They are a good group on the whole and h enjoys working with them. But three out of the 24 never complete their coursework on tim He's tried getting everyone to do it in class so that he can oversee and support them, b these three learners still get very little done. They're not friends and they don't sit togeth so it's not about them distracting one another. It's not about ability either, as far as he c see. They're all reasonably able, and the coursework is certainly not beyond their ability complete. They just don't seem motivated. Miles has tried telling them they're going to the course if they don't start putting some effort in, but it hasn't made any difference. It's even that they misbehave. They don't. They just don't do anything. Miles has no idea wh going on or what to try next.

advice'. You arrive at the school where you are met by a senior member of staff. She tells you that you won't have all of the Year 11s at your presentation because *there's no point the brighter ones being there*. You feel quite cross about this and resolve to say something about it later. You're led to a classroom where about 25 pupils are waiting for you. They listen attentively to what you have to say. You've made a point of putting together an interesting and lively presentation and you're pleased to see that you've engaged their interest. At the end of ten minutes you invite questions. They're a long time coming, but eventually one pupil puts her hand up and says, *So college can help you get into university?*

That's right, you tell her.

I thought you could only get to university if they let you stay on at school.

You explain again that there is an alternative, vocationally-orientated route into higher education. It's quite clear from the questions that follow that FE has been presented to these pupils as a more practical and easier option for those who *aren't very good at maths or English* or *don't do very well in exams*. By the time you've finished you're hoping you've gone some way towards persuading them otherwise. Now, you think, it's time to have a word with that teacher; explain to her a thing or two.

» You want to explain to the teacher where some of her mistaken notions come from. What aspects of FE's background and history might it be useful to explain to her?

» You would also like her to understand how these notions of hers are perpetuated and reinforced. What arguments would you draw on in order to explain this to her?

Using these themes and arguments in assignments

As well as using your understanding of FE to analyse and address practical situations and incidents, you'll also be expected to demonstrate a grasp of this contextual background in any coursework you're required to do as part of your initial training or continuing development. We're going to look at two examples of how people have done this. The first is by a trainee teacher who is expected to write a rationale or explanation of the lesson plan she has prepared for a session in which she is to be observed and assessed by her tutor. The second is part of an MA assignment written by a teacher in his first year of professional practice. Notice how they build these key themes and arguments into their work to support and explain the points they are making.

SAMPLE ASSIGNMENT EXTRACT 1

Justification of a lesson plan

As my lesson plan shows, I will begin this session with a short quiz which allows the learners and myself to recap what we covered in the previous lesson. This is partly a confidence-building exercise, and it's absolutely necessary because so many of the learners in this group have little faith in their own abilities. There are two possible reasons for this. The first is that their own history of failure in school may have undermined their belief that they can succeed. The second is that there is a common belief that FE is for less able learners, and because these learners are here they assume they must not be very good at learning. This assumption about FE is an idea that got associated with it a long time ago, when vocational training was thought of as a second-best option and only suitable for the lower classes in society. This idea still persists with some people today because of the way it gets reinforced. The most able learners in school get steered towards A levels and university. They tend not to come into FE. So FE is still seen as a second-best choice. It's a vicious circle. Therefore one of the main aims of my lesson planning is to address this, and so building up learners' confidence and interest underlies most of my planning decisions.

For example, I make sure there is a lot of activity where learners are actively engaged rather than simply sitting listening to me. This is why I have chosen as my methods for this lesson case studies, small group discussion and simulations. All of these activities allow me to observe whether the outcomes are being met, and they operate with me in a facilitator role so that I can circulate, support and advise and make sure no individual or group gets stuck or loses pace or interest. In planning my time, I've made sure that no one activity lasts longer than 15 minutes, which is about the maximum attention span I can reasonably expect from them. I've aimed to get a balance between stretching them a little but not undermining their confidence. So, for example, in activity 4 I don't expect them to make their own notes from scratch. I provide them with a framework where they can fill in the key words, and so build up their confidence gradually.

My plan also contains a 'Plan B'. This is a set of alternative activities that I can bring into play if I notice learners becoming disengaged. Disengagement is a natural consequence of their low sense of self-esteem. It's not that they are 'bad'. I've seen from observing other teachers that getting angry with learners who won't engage doesn't address the issue at all. It just undermines their sense of self-advocacy even further and makes the problem worse. But a quick and snappy change of activity often does work.

» Which key debates and theories is this trainee teacher drawing on here?

» In your view, does she argue her case well? Are there any changes you think she should make before she gives this rationale to her tutor? What questions do you think her tutor might ask her about it?

» She hasn't cited any sources to support her argument. Looking back to the relevant chapters, identify which sources she could have referred to here (not counting this book).

SAMPLE ASSIGNMENT EXTRACT 2

MA assignment, 'The impact of policy change on your institution'

Background

The market in education underlies many of the policy changes that have impacted on FE in the past 20 years. Presenting education and training as a commodity inevitably changes the purpose and meaning of teaching (Ball, 1993). There are two observable symptoms of this that have had an impact on my college. One is the reluctance of schools to retain or recruit less able learners. The other is the widening gap between the purposes and aims of teachers and those of senior management. Teachers are first and foremost concerned with supporting learning. Their agenda is to do with pedagogic practice. Senior management, on the other hand, are required to focus on corporate issues such as competition, profit and loss. Their decision-making has to be finance-led, rather than curriculum led. We have, therefore, within the college, two different agendas. The existence of what might sometimes be conflicting goals within one institution can create difficulties and tensions. It also means that curriculum change can only realistically be driven from the top down, and this usually means with the prime motive of competing effectively in the education and training market, rather than from motives based on sound pedagogic principles. An example here is the dominance in FE of competence-based courses which impose a narrow model of what learning is about and exclude the possibility of a more liberal curriculum (Pring, 1999), and also, it has been argued, fail to provide the excitement or stimulation necessary to maintain learner engagement (Wolf, 2007).

» What are the main arguments that this teacher drawing on here?

» In your view, does she cite sources in the appropriate places to support what she is saying?

» How would you summarise her argument in one sentence?

» In what ways is this extract written differently from the one before? Identify at least two features which identify this as written for 'scholarly' rather than professional purposes.

SAMPLE ASSIGNMENT EXTRACT 3

Initial Teacher Training Assignment, 'Observation of an experienced teacher'

Introduction

The teacher I observed has been teaching at the college for five years. I observed her teaching a very mixed class of learners. It was mixed in terms of age – there were some quite mature adults in there as well younger learners of 17 or 18. It was also mixed in terms of ability. Some of the learners had skills that others didn't, such as the ability to take useful notes, but some had quite low level literacy skills. There was a roughly equal mix of male and female. The older, adult learners also had more knowledge and experience that they could draw on. The teacher's main challenge, as far as I could see, was to plan and teach a lesson that would engage all the learners and make sure none felt bored because it was too easy or anxious and excluded because it was too difficult for them.

On the lesson plan this teacher had included a column headed 'Differentiation'. In this she had included what she called 'extension tasks' to challenge the more able or informed learners, and 'peer supported tasks' to provide support for those who needed more help. This seemed a very good idea to me, and she operated it in practice in a way that wouldn't make any of the learners think of themselves as the 'A' group or the 'B' group.

I know from my reading that this mix of learners, presenting a wide range of learning needs, is characteristic of FE. One of the reasons for this is that FE offers such a wide range of qualifications, from basic level to degrees. But I didn't expect to find such a range within one class. The teacher explained to me that this mix is largely because of the FE demographic (the sort of learners the sector recruits). Adults often return to education or training via FE, bringing their life and work experience, which teachers can tap into as a resource. And at the same time, school leavers come into FE to get qualifications for their chosen career, keen to learn but with little life experience. And thirdly there are school leavers who enter the sector a bit reluctantly, not having done very well at school and sometimes lacking any study skills or enthusiasm for learning. I'd never thought of this before. But she's right. And it does make a very challenging mix. I really admired the way this teacher got the older learners talking about their experiences of work. You could see it got the younger ones interested because it was 'real life' and not just teacher talk.

» How could this trainee teacher have expanded further on his explanation of the diverse learning needs of this class?

» It would have been useful if he had given some examples of the 'extension tasks' and 'peer supported tasks' that the teacher included in her lesson plan. He could then have evaluated later in his assignment how these seemed to work in practice. What sort of activities do you imagine would be appropriate under these headings?

Ways forward: what teachers can do

Already in this chapter we've heard about two teacher who've been thinking carefully about what they can do to meet the needs of their learners and build up their confidence. (Sample assignment extracts 1 and 3.) The first teacher's summary of the situation she faces is a useful one. Let's just look at it again. She says:

...so many of the learners in this group have little faith in their own abilities. There are two possible reasons for this. The first is that their own history of failure in school may have undermined their belief that they can succeed. The second is that there is a common belief that FE is for less able learners, and because these learners are here they assume they must not be very good at learning.

She's flagging up two possible causes here, both clearly linked in what we could call a feed-back loop that perpetuates the problem. We explored this theme from various angles in Chapters 1, 2, 5, 7 and 8. The teacher who is planning her lesson here – let's call her Raisa – is very clear about what this demands of the teacher. She argues convincingly that teachers can and should take these complex issues into account both when planning lessons and when making sense of learner disengagement.

She's not alone here. In Chapter 9 we heard from teachers and learners who spoke enthu-siastically about the impact that FE teachers can have on the confidence and self-image of their learners. A great deal of what they said there was about interpersonal relationships and establishing mutual respect. This is all evidence that teachers really can make a difference.

Critical Thinking Activity 2

» Go back to Chapter 9 and make a list of ways in which teachers can have a positive impact on the confidence of learners.

» Now add to the list those planning points described by Raisa in this chapter. You should now have a set of at least six ideas.

» Now write these as action points. How many of them do you already incorporate into your everyday teaching?

» Now add at least one more of your own: something additional you can do to improve even further the way in which you support the confidence and engagement of your learners.

Ways forward: policy and practice

Although we recognise that, as teachers, one of our primary responsibilities is to support our learners in this way, it is also important that the college in which we're working has systems and policies which help rather than hinder us. We've encountered some examples of good practice: for example, the college referred to by Experienced Teacher 2 in the previous chap-ter, which made sure that new recruits received careful counselling and advice so that they could be allocated a place on a course that would suit their needs.

Critical Thinking Activity 3

» Think carefully about the recurring themes we've encountered in this book – themes about status, purpose, esteem, behaviour, attainment, and the language that we use – and consider how your current college addresses these. Look specifically at:

a) *internal policies relating to learners and learning;*

b) *support systems and services which are in place for learners;*

c) *recruitment practices.*

» If the college principal were to ask you for your view on what could be done further, what one suggestion would you make? On what grounds would you justify it? And what evidence would you be able to present to support your suggestion?

Chapter reflections

We began this chapter with a summary of the themes and arguments that have been central to this book, including the question of parity and choice; the social origins and subsequent status of FE; the vocational curriculum; the root causes of disengagement and negative behaviour; teachers' role and responsibilities; and government policies and their impact on the language of FE. This was followed by a series of case studies that helped us to look at how we can apply these ideas to help us gain a fuller understanding of practical situations and dilemmas. Then we looked at how this knowledge and understanding can be incorporated into assignments and other work required for your teaching qualification or continuing professional development. And finally you were asked to reflect on ways forward – what you and your college can do to make learners' experience of FE even better.

Taking it further

In order to keep up to date with developments in the sector – and, as you know, there's *always* something – it's a good idea to keep an eye on key websites, including the government's websites for education and training, the FE Guild, and the *Times Educational Supplement* (*TES*) website's FE section.

Department of Education (UK), www.education.gov.uk

Department of Education (Northern Ireland), www.deni.gov.uk

Department of Business, Innovation and Skills, www.gov.uk/goverment/organisations/department-for-business-innovation-skills

Information on the Education and Training Foundation (formerly FE Guild) can be accessed through the Institute for Learning website, www.ifl.ac.uk

Times Education Supplement FE Focus, www.tes.co.uu/topSection.aspx? navCode=507

Index